Table of Contents

Stonewall's Legacy

Edited by
Marc Rosen and Rita "Rusty" Rose

Forewords

Having read submissions for *Stonewall's Legacy*, I beamed with pride.
Within the many pages are poems from talented poets. The writings represent the best of our
vibrant rainbow and also showcase our diversity and unity.
You will find there is something for everyone in this anthology.
Please enjoy and share it with your friends.
As a modern day pioneer of the LGBTQIA movement,
I am honored to have been asked to serve as editor of this fine historical anthology.
I am also proud to know my participation at the Stonewall Rebellion '69 has been embraced by future generations.
I pass this torch with affection and confidence.

Thank you.
In Solidarity, love and light,
Rita 'Rusty' Rose

I don't know what else I can say that Rita hasn't already put so succinctly. When I came out at age 18, it was to a combination of "stop shoving it in our faces!" and "congratulations, nobody cares!" While relieved that I wouldn't have to fear being disowned or worse, I didn't exactly get a coming out party either. I spent the next twelve years searching for community, a sense of safety, possibly even some sort of assurance that I was wanted and welcome. It took a while, but I eventually found most of that, especially after meeting my co-editor, Rita, and reconnecting with our people's history and heritage.

Stonewall's Legacy was born out of this constant search, this need to connect and belong, to honor our past, present, and future, bound into a single volume. In that spirit, we strove to ensure that this anthology represents our community's myriad faces, our hope, our grief, the terror that gripped us in the AIDS crisis, our desperate struggle for the faint dream that some day, all of these struggles will be outdated, and nobody will bat an eye at who or what we are. That's why they rebelled at Stonewall. That's why we continue to rebel. Long live the Rebellion and longer live its Legacy. I promise, none of it was in vain.

With love,
Marc Rosen

To the Stonewall Pioneers and Stonewall Veterans:
You rebelled against our oppressors fifty years ago
So that we could have reason to celebrate today.
Your sacrifices and struggles will never be forgotten.

To all the heirs of Stonewall's Legacy:
They rebelled for our sake, and it isn't over yet
It's our turn to carry the torch, burning now for fifty years
From Stonewall to Pulse
WeHo to Hell's Kitchen
Bayard Rustin to Laverne Cox
Sylvia Rivera to Chelsea Manning
Linda Rhodes to Wanda Sykes

And all others who spur us to action
We will live. We will love. We will prevail.

(From both of us)

Special thanks to

The Stonewall Rebellion Veterans' Association, for their endorsement
and blessing
Lambda Literary, for their wide-reaching distribution of our call for
submissions
LGBTQ centers across the country, for their life-saving and life-
essential work
You, the reader. We entrust you to keep the flame burning for us.

(From Rusty)

To many friends/pioneers, both living and deceased, who were equally
courageous in rebelling with me at the Stonewall Inn, during the wee
hours of the first night.
Prayers and courage to members in our community who have died,
live in fear, or are confined somewhere in the world—you are not
forgotten.
Thank you to Marc Rosen, my friend, with whom I have brainstormed
with to bring this anthology to fruition.
To my daughter, Melanie and niece, Nicole and love to all friends and
supporters everywhere.
And last but not least, a big woof goes out to Ralphie and Button Rose,
my Dachshund companions!

(From Marc)

To Rick, for all your help and support towards the end of this project,
including helping us promote
To Pam, for your efforts to tell Rusty's story at long last, as it always
should have been
To our many eager contributors, I hope you're proud of how far we've
come
Thank you to Rusty Rose, my dear friend and mentor, for taking me
under your wing
To our people who died in the AIDS endemic, at the hands of fascist
regimes,
Or who endure a living death in institutions, nursing homes, and other
human warehouses,
I yearn for you to receive justice and freedom

Lindsay Agins

<u>Longing</u>

In a room full of women
Drinks on the bar
Pocket full of money
Sky full of stars
There's only one thing
For which I starve
To live by your side
To die in your arms

Joel Allegretti

<u>The Man-Rat</u>

> After Robert Mapplethorpe's
> *Self Portrait with Whip (1978)*

I'm the spitting image of a king-
Size Manhattan rat. Ever wonder

If there are queer rats? I mean little
Bitch rats that like to take a bull rat's

Hard rat dick in their pinprick rat ass.
Rat-fucks on a West 14th St. loading

Dock, sharing the meatpacking hours
With trash-blond Gansevoort queens

Hopping in and out of '75 Camaros
With Jersey plates. Bottom rats rat-

Squeaking in unlubricated-anal-sex
Agony/ecstasy when the pumping

Rat cocks spurt threads of hot rat
Cum in the open-all-night rat holes.

Top and bottom rats in post-climax
Collapse. The bitch rats running off

To pick up other bull rats, chattering
In whatever passes for queer-rat code,

"Fuck my rat ass into jelly." Now,
That's what I call giving a rat's ass.

Rachel Antrobus

<u>A Winter Romance</u>

Take my hand in yours
lead me forward
Forward through the snow suffocating
the earth below
Guide me to that secret place you found
when no one was around

The forest is a shelter now
trees huddling together to protect us
from the cold night air
Your mother doesn't know you left your
light on
doesn't know you aren't home
She would never guess you were here
with me
not your oldest friend

She came in once when we were kids
planning our wedding
She asked why there were two brides
concern already clouding her eyes
But we didn't see it then
we just knew we wanted a joint wedding
Back then we thought there would be
two grooms as well

My hand is still in yours as you squeeze
drawing my attention back to the path you're
leading me down
You look back
eyes aglow
as you promise we're almost there

We reach the oak you told me
about the day before
The one you carved our initials into
You didn't want to risk our names
not so close to where we live
but L and S is enough

I stroke my fingertips over the gouges
in the bark
and you do the same
Till our hands meet and
you twine our fingers
palm to palm

And then we're lip to lip as you
push me into the tree where you
immortalised us
The pressure a relief I hope leaves
scars
Anything real
tangible for me to hold on to

But as the trees betray us
the cold seeps in
Our bodies start to shake
and I know before you say it
we are about to part
And the countdown will start again
everyday an endless torture till I know
if I can see you again

Back here in this secret place you claimed as ours
or somewhere we're yet to make our own
All I know is I dream of summer
because finding time to be with you in this
bitter cold is becoming impossible

<u>Silenced Epiphanies</u>

In In the deep deep dead
of the deep deep night
I realised
I fantasised

a boy in one eye,
    a girl in the other

I work up my breaths
and a moan follows
an exhalation
but not relief.

Afterwards,
I push down what I know
bury it
down deep
      in that
            deep
              deep
                  night
And think about boys till I
                  see the light.

Con Artist

<u>Taking Her To The Cross</u>

It was the title of the painting
that hung on the wall before me...

Two women embraced in a passionate Argentine tango...

This was not a religious matter...

You could see in the background the beautiful Central Park bridge
...but no one was crossing it...

...or maybe one woman is coming out...
crossing over as a lesbian...

Alas...it is a term in Argentine tango,
when the leader gently takes the follower to the cross...

...wherein the follower is gracefully compelled
to cross their feet at the ankle...

Taking her to the cross should never make her cross!

Elliot Ayres

<u>Where I have learned to say my name</u>

Some people believe
That every decision you make
Leads to the creation of another universe
So one world exists to contain each outcome.

If that's true, then there are billions of worlds that exist for me.
One where I never start T,
One where I never change my name,
One where I allow myself suffocation.

Still, I hope that they're right.
I hope that there are infinite worlds
Because the only thing that could comfort me
Is alternate versions of myself.

It would help me fall asleep to know
That somewhere out there
I will learn how to breathe,
To just breathe and just be.

Somewhere out there,
I haven't given up.
I'll be fluent in myself and the parts that make me
Until they become my first language.

There, I can scream out what has been weighing on my chest
Though I would have no need to.
It would flow like music outward
And everyone would know what I need them to hear.

In that separate universe,
I have no need to prove myself
And all the evidence for who I am
Is as visible as the scars across my chest.

There, I pray only to the person who I am going to become
The only one with all the answers
The only one who knows
That sometimes everything unfolds exactly as it should.

In one world I have felt the ocean turn in my stomach.
But in another, I have steady hands,
Ones that no longer shake
And whose tired calluses have worn into soft skin.

In that world, my name will finally bring me home
To sit in outer space, where I will fit among the stars
Or on the Earth where I began
To learn how to become.

While I'm here, I will figure out how to rearrange the stars in own
galaxy.
I will remind myself that the ground exists beneath my feet
As surely as stardust fuels my heartbeat
Until my own world learns to say my name.

Ellen Bass

<u>The Small Country</u>

Unique, I think, is the Scottish *tartle*, that hesitation
when introducing someone whose name you've forgotten

And what could capture *cafuné*, the Brazilian Portuguese way to say
running your fingers, tenderly, through someone's hair?

Is there a term in any tongue for choosing to be happy?

And where is speech for the block of ice we pack in the sawdust of our
hearts?

What appellation approaches the smell of apricots thickening the air
when you boil jam in early summer?

What words reach the way I touched you last night—
as though I had never known a woman—an explorer,
wholly curious to discover each particular
fold and hollow, without guide,
not even the mirror of my own body.

Last night you told me you liked my eyebrows.
You said you never really noticed them before.
What is the word that fuses this freshness
with the pity of having missed it.

And how even touch cannot mean the same to both of us,
even in this small country of our bed,
even in this language with only two native speakers.

Sally Bellerose

Married Ladies Have Sex in the Bathroom 1975

We did it everywhere.
We were middle aged women
with middle aged husbands
and school aged children.

Mostly in daylight.
Mostly in twenty minutes
or less.
In places so common
they'd never suspect.

Every room of both houses,
the cellar,
the garage,
the neighbors' children's four foot wading pool.

And then there were the bathrooms,
the bathrooms,
the bathrooms of Fitzwillies,
         the GirlsClub,
         Caldor's,
         Shoprite,
         the bushes
in back of the bar at the end of the street.

We did it on my picnic table,
and under her picnic table.
We did it in extremes,
dressed for inclement weather.

Coming, fully clothed,
hats,
scarves,
boots,

and mittens.
Coming, buck screaming naked,
in the hot dirt,
of some God forsaken road,
with bugs crawling,
in woods that never gave back
her pink lace panties.

We did it lying flat
on the kitchen floor,
our heads pressing up against the kitchen door.
Our bodies barring our boy's entrance.

We did it seated
in my car, moving,
in her car, in the body shop,
at the airport,
on the plane to Baltimore
while she calmly discussed
Women, War, and Peace
with another woman in the next seat.
In the hot tubs,
even though I hate the hot tubs.
On the stairs outside the hot tubs,
not waiting for the couple inside
to come out.

We did it with phones ringing,
kids screaming,
dogs barking,
tubs overflowing,
and dinner burning in the pot.
We did it with fingers so hot
we thought sure we'd be branded forever.

We did it with bodies so tired,
hearts so heavy,
that doin it was the last thing
on our minds.

Still, something greedy whispered,
get it while you can girls,
because you never know
if or when
you're gonna get again.

We did it and called it empowerment,
lust,
avarice,
and adultery.
We dared man or nature
to deny that doin it
was anything but sacred.

We flaunted.
We hid.
Tense and tangled,
sometimes we forgot
when to run, when to taunt.

We stopped.
Caught our breaths, confronted.
Like dogs in heat, we fought.
Our lives uprooted,
recovered to fight,
to blame some more.

In the end
we cared for ourselves
(and others)
enough to stay
alive, in this world, together.
And a year,
and a year,
and the years go by.
Less and less
we press each other.
Still we love.
But oh the sex.

It's never been the same.
Life on the edge is an addiction.
Honest life is pleasant,
better, definitely better,
but so damned tame.

Prior publication credits:
"Married Ladies Have Sex in the Bathroom", *The Poetry of Sex*, edited by Tee Corrine, Banned Books, 1992.
"Married Ladies Have Sex in the Bathroom", *Women on Women 2*, edited by Naomi Haloch and Joan Nestle, Plume, June 1993.
"Married Ladies Have Sex in the Bathroom", *My Lover is a Woman*, edited by Leslea Newman, Ballantine Books, 1996.
"Married Ladies," *Best Bisexual Erotica*, Edited by Bill Brent and Carol Queen, Black Books, 2002.
"Married Ladies," *Lady Business*, Edited by Bryon Borland, Sibling Rivalry Press, 2013
"Married Ladies," *Best Bisexual Erotica: Best of the Best Reissue*, Cleis Press, 2015.

Raymond Berry

<u>Harbinger</u>

For Robyn

The times my door kicked in
By you, the prophet
Predicting my death
Because I took it up the ass
Each time, I forgave
Until something triggered you again
This time, rage, because I agreed
With the Jacksons attending the BET awards

After Michael's death
Telling me to shut up
That's why you have *AIDS,*
What's that? my nephews asked
Ask your uncle.
God is killing him, you said
How you really felt
That day in the hospital

Your prophecy finally happening
Your first words, a question
If I could share forks or straws
We'll buy separate plates
I'm okay, I thought
Because you didn't ask
Cabinets stacked with plastic
And other disposables

Like me, you said,
Used once and tossed away
I understood now
Why gay men didn't tell their families
Because Even in death

They knew
Loved ones, like you, my twin,
Would take their hurt and load it

<u>truvada</u>

200mg emtricitabine (em-trye-SYE-ta-been)/300 mg tenofovir disoproxil fumarate (te-NOE-fo-veer dye-soe-PROX-ill FYOU-mar-ate)/30 tablets/take one tablet each night at bedtime/ideally with food/possible risks/lactic acidosis/buffalo hump/insomnia/high glucose levels/excess gas/inflammation of pancreas/itching/headache/liver and kidney disorders/ decrease in neutrophil/ anemia/ difficulty breathing/bones and muscles ache/everything i eat goes through me

<u>Equilibrium</u>

cd4 normalizes, cells quit attacking own
weight returns, cheeks become full
no night sweats or brown-stained sheets
every scar fades
limbs less numb
strength comes back full
meals eaten without releasing, coffee without gas
all because of one injection
magic liquid needled under flesh
and
scarecrows return to human
touch once more without the prayer
leave toothbrush and razor next to sink
no separate china for family visits
because we are who we were
before death erased us

<u>How We Once Were</u>

for Aaron

Whole things
Bodies now betrayed by illness
So light
We can't feel the wreckage:

My cd4: 0
Your liver: recalcitrant
We overlook our fragility
You graduated college

I survived my first decade
How lucky we were
To be once whole things
The body a thing of its own

You coughing blood during my final
Me losing every t-cell
Us half a self
Reticent in our trajectory

Like a stem in a stump
We grow and blossom in rock
Blooming still
But not quite the same

<u>AIDS Litany</u>

I buried a life I was not supposed to have has swallowed me, and I lie
awake each night and praise the memory—
I praise the few T cells left
The cuts that heal, and the ones that need more time
I praise Atripla for being one instead of three
My blood for not asking why
Inflammation that settles, thrush for not returning
I praise men for leaving, my first for saying nothing lasts
I praise the one who did pull out
My hole for keeping in bowels
Washrooms for being close
I praise the day for its distractions
Side effects for sensation
My mother for teaching me to keep one eye open
I praise my father for showing how quickly men disappear
I praise the ancestors for being
I praise Sustiva for vampire dreams
I praise chat lines for phone bones
My body for refusing weight
I praise Bush and Reagan for ignoring the problem
Healthcare for excluding us, social security for nothing
I praise ADAP for rejection, life insurance for denials
I praise X-tube, the only free get-off site
I praise support groups for their judgment
My viral load almost undetectable
My liver and kidneys, thyroid for the effort
I praise PrEP for being too late
Scruff and Grindr for the status box
Everyone for not being stigma free
I praise Chicago for the only marathon
I praise the red ribbon, long forgotten
I praise the Olympic bid for coming first
I praise blacks for becoming the new face
I praise my seed for being tainted
My shame for whispering
And I praise the truth for not being enough

*Atripla is a one-pill cocktail used to treat HIV; Prep is a regimen that prevents HIV in HIV- people

24

Michael Gray Bulla

<u>I Go To The Movies With A Boy</u>

for the first time and I think
the world might collapse into itself.
We stand in the concession line and my
fingertips tremble with something—a
desire for touch / and a fear for it,
the lingering stare of the audience,
the performance I am always putting / on

because yes, here we are,
and I tug at my button down and wonder
if the whole town can tell what I am / what
we are and if so, if there is anybody
here who cares enough to do something
about it.

So we stand there. So we're breathing,
and the line creeps ever forward. My hand
is so much smaller in this moment than I
want it to be / need it to be;

if I clenched it in a fist would that
keep away the violence?

Yes, maybe,
or no, possibly,
or I will hope I do not have to find out but I
am finding out the other parts:

how the fist keeps him from reaching for me,
how he might know what I am thinking or maybe
think it too;

and oh, how we stand with our arms at our sides,
afraid for / of / one another and the weight of touch;

how the distance between our shoulders is so far,
and I am only thinking the entire time
they must know, they must know;

and every face I pass is a potential instigator,
a bible verse with consonants that sound
like gunshots / blessings that become an AR-15
the moment I turn my head and there are so many
that I fear chewing through the bullets.

So I lose the touch / so I don't look around,
and the line moves up another foot and I
tug at my button down and wait
for the three words—six / if you have the patience—

the same way I am still waiting for hellfire to rain down
and drench me for my sins, sear away my skin and bones until
it is just the treading part of me—

and our hands sway at our sides, palm
trees in a storm, silent casualties of a culture
that forces a clenched fist. We say nothing,

and my fingertips are
still trembling.

<u>To The Girls Who They Say Converted Me</u>

The womb of your life is vacant
but I still think about you every now and then.
Even with the lights on you were never
him and I
wasn't sure how I felt about that.
You pressed a sweaty palm to my own
while a stoner breathed smoke over my other shoulder.
In an empty theater only four
sat in the audience and she
told me her name was Natalia.
Her womb was not a womb but a
battleground; a heaven; a plight.
You,
clumsy in your speech and frightened in your flirting
asked me why I never said anything back.
I told you I wasn't sure but not
that I never would be.

You never did get to tell me your name
but I read it sometimes,
from friends,
blinking back at me from the cracked screen of my phone,
telling me that *you have changed her name to Daniella*
and I do not miss the change in pronouns, either.

I still wonder how you're doing.

Guillermo Filice Castro

<u>Can We Get Home In One Piece Please</u>

— After the Pulse Club attack

I want to scream in my sleep.
I latch every door
in the block as if each led
to my bedroom. All the ghosts
I've tongued
on the dance floor
are here. If only they'd let me
speak without a
mouth. If only they could
speak. Once
rounds and shots
meant just drinks. Please
I want to scream,
cornered by skidding tires
and high beams
into a dark lot.
I wait. I pounce.
My knife goes into the killer's belly
repeatedly and bloodlessly,
metal goring grimy sand.
More than ever
I am not an animal of peace.
Not now.
The night under my hooves
cools and clinks,
empty of stars.

<u>Citizens</u>

Two guys walk into a bar.
Two gay guys. Into a straight bar.
Lovers. With enough money for a beer each.
Over a shared hot dog
the younger one had proposed:
We gotta meet women! And out
they went in their innocently foreign sandals.
Sorry to bother you,
the older partner addressed the bartender,
but do you have any friends
who might want to marry us, um,
for the papers?
The bartender draws back,
her torso a bridge pulling away
from a tall ship in flames. She looks up,
closes her eyes. As if actually
mulling over that question
while stretched under a legal sun.
Her only two customers next to her,
their hunger naked, horizontal. As waves
roll in the distance. As birds
notarize with their footprints
a brown document of sand,
citizens suited for flight.
The bartender shakes her head *No*.
Queen of her island of shot glasses
that turn throats into tiny volcanoes.
Where rings left by bottles on coasters
fade faster than a crazy marriage proposal.
Stamps on passports with overstayed visas.
Punchlines no one laughs at
beneath palm trees dangling green cards.

Bésame Mucho

There's a slick anthem
we like to belt, my friend and I.

Each to undo a set of lips,

rings for the girth
of his breath and mine. Flesh

as spice, as prodigy
in bed:

Join us,
cotton to us.

We like to rule big.
Grab, let go, nip;

then plan our own overthrow.

Flesh as flag, ablaze.
Oh homo-land—I'll

map you out
in whatever tissue

I spit his seed in.

<u>Before April</u>

*On April 2, 1982 war began between Argentina and England
over control of the Malvinas/Falkland Islands.*

When we couldn't stop
Calling Sergeant Romero
A fag behind his back
While he yelled it to our faces

Before the colonel's own face turned red
During his morning harangue
When to his eyes we had become a gang
Of effeminates

Before the English came

Before we shouldered ammunition into long cargo trains
And fed pastries to the open pockets on our sorry fatigues

Before the English sunk ships

We lay on our backs

After our swim
After you stopped me
From pissing in the water tank

People still have to drink that

After climbing up
on narrow rungs unfit
for bare feet

Far above our fellow soldiers
We lay on our backs
Listening to the enemy's music

Woozy as the breeze that raised your nipples
And missed mine

The light so bright with eyes closed
We saw red, only red

To The Woman in Me

That you once looked like Georgia O'Keefe, blame it on the

       Halloween makeup.

Neither beauty nor heavy-breasted beast—

You're still sweet, baby, armed with ripped pink pantyhose as I imagine.

But if you had rather go by unnoticed, not make a sound, let me know. Right,

I've denied you before, lips Revlon raw in the tiny mirror.

Then the sudden shame, Mother's compact snapping shut

on the whole shebang. One midsummer night in the mid-eighties

you leaned against my friend's door, a demure and bearded young lady in

       a perm wig.

On a dare you stepped out to strut along the long distance trucks

parked beneath the froufrou of leaves in the dark.

The cat calls made you squirm and return inside to uncork more wine and
       cap the fear.

It was fun you said to the gaggle of giggling men in drag. Dress or no

       dress, Georgia,

please come out, be my tomboyish bride. I'll throw myself

under your jaunty cowboy boots like rain or glitter

on some outrageous rooftop, if you ask.

Rob Colgate

<u>Homecoming</u>

Sweet ghost of moon sweet ghost
of home
Sweet ghost singing the moon
Sweet ghost of moon sweet ghost
of singing

We sing panic we sing hallelujah
We sing for the boys without ghosts
We sing for the boys without sweetness

I have been a sweet boy in the night
I sing for the boys
I sing for home
Sing for years and years
Sing panic sing

Sweet ghost sing a hole into my side
Sweet ghost sing a river into its gushing
Sweet ghost sing a bullet into the night
Sweet ghost sing a sanctified geyser

Moonsweet geyser I am not home
Moonsweet geyser I am not here
Sweet ghost sing for years and years

Boys with no moon
                be sweet
Boys with no hallelujah
                sing panic

Sweetness in the night
Ghosts in the boys
Sing

Sweet panic walks the river and sings
Sweet panic walks the river and sings
Sweet panic sings
the river

Sweet ghost of moon sing panic to me
Sweet ghost of moon sing panic to me

Sweet ghost of moon sweet ghost
of home
Sweet ghost singing the moon
Sweet ghost of moon sweet ghost
of singing

Sweet boy without ghost
                a hole in my side

<u>Sestina for a New York City Gay Bar</u>

"Nightlife in NYC may always be in flux, but for the LGBTQ community, some places will always be home." – TimeOut magazine, 2018

Walking to therapy
with a monster
in me, a pain rises
from nowhere.
Inside, boxers
pummel me to pieces.

I lose my pieces
and skip therapy,
grab extra boxers
and outrun the monster,
jump on the train to nowhere
to catch you before sunrise.

In the light of some high-rise
you tell me about those pieces
of yours that have nowhere
to go. I'm sorry. I ask about therapy.
You don't answer. The monster
in between us leaves his boxers

on at night. We climb into our boxes
and fight to be the last to rise.
In the morning you pour the monster
juice; I sit next to him, cereal pieces
floating in milk like dead bodies. Therapy
is closed on Sunday so we go nowhere.

"You know we're going nowhere.
You put your life into boxes,
that's why you're in therapy."
You get a rise
out of me and my pieces.

I don't know who the monster

is anymore. This monster
is going nowhere.
You scatter all my pieces,
I run outside in my boxers
and scream until the hairs rise
on the necks of the people in therapy.

I grab the pieces of the monster
that rise to the surface, shove them into boxes,
meet you over in nowhere or therapy.

<u>He</u>

i. Land

Gabe was the land the earth
beneath my feet he was a mountain he
was tall he was cold he was tense
he was a battle between the ground
and itself he lost the battle but held
his ground I caught him

at his peak I got off the bus and
watched his words avalanche
pile up into something worth
digging into so I dug
and into him I went I became

a hike I hiked through his treeline
I gasped for breath grasped
for something all he gave me was
starlight and I was nightmared
he rumbled when I strayed
from the path so I stayed

to the path he could not get
past the valley I could not get
through the pass the ground fell out
from underneath me we fell out Gabe
let me fall he was two plates shifted
I took a breath drifted out of his path.

ii. Ocean

I fell into the ocean of Thomas
and nearly drowned he was so
dark it was so deep I thought
it was supposed to be cool
and blue but not this water
not this boy he ripped me

in as soon as I had tiptoed
to the shore I lost sight of land
lost sight of sky lost my sight
in the undertow he got under me
towed me past where the sun

could find us the sun could not
find us it lost us and I let myself get
lost the ocean took me by the ankles
and tossed me the tide and the current
got me the whirlpools engulfed me

he ravaged me pumped my lungs until
they were filled with him then
spit me up on the beach
Thomas spit on me I coughed
and coughed until I could breathe
without tasting the salt his salt his salt.

iii. Sky

And Matt he was the sky and I
owe him everything for that
he was everything that moved me
moved around me the air the light
the wind the space where I existed

when he became the sky I could not
exist without him he surrounded me
made me float I was wrapped in him
I was a part of him I was a cloud
he kissed me with rain and lightning

I soaked up every touch every motion
he was a part of me but he pushed
me around pulled me apart how
could I hold myself together if
he was every breeze every gust

I trusted him but he cried and I fell
to the ground Matt could not hold me
anymore hold me up anymore so I tore
from the sky but with every breath
I take I still feel him in me.

Steven Cordova

<u>Booked</u>

I couldn't be at the riots.
I was six and living in
a city not The City.

I feel like I was at the riots—
sometimes I feel I was.
Could it be it's in the blood?

If not, how is it I slip on blood
running toward sirens? Or feel the sun going down
then coming up again

on the first then the sixth day
of the riots?
Could it be you're never too young to riot?

Or that blood's more
than something received from mom and pops?—
that blood's something that'll pop

up off a yellowing page,
the black and white pictures,
a riot of texts?

<u>History Repeats Itself</u>

A ROCK by any other name's a stone.
Handcuffs, like SCISSORS, cut.
Borders are PAPER-thin

At Stonewall Inns,
ROCK crushes SCISSORS,
PAPER sooths ROCK.

Repeat this
cuff by brick, brick by cuff,
again and again.

Alfred Corn

<u>Young Soldier</u>

Straight lines make for classic manly features
(softened a little by the curving cheekbones).
Magnetism of his eyes, blue-green
landing lights that beam relaxed assurance
from under an overhang of soot-black brows,
the left cast in the rôle of circumflex.
Beard roughly the same black, his lower lip
exposed—a plump and chewable sherbet pink.
No way, though, to elude his rock-steady
gaze, lit up with just the faintest spark
of mischief. Which must come from knowing why
spectators blink and almost gasp—as he may
have done the day his dialogue with the mirror
confirmed the ugly-duckling years were over.

Always wondered how it would feel to be
a world-class model, tall, broad-shouldered,
arms articulate, a sculpted chest
with fine pelt charcoaled in by a master draftsman.
Well, here's the opportunity to ask!
He shakes his head and says he never much
thinks about it. Instead, returns the serve:
"So, Mister Poet, you tell *me* what it's like
to hook up pretty words the way *you* do.'
"Oh. Sorry. I can't really answer that one.
Maybe if we… just shut up and get to work?"

Mobius Strip

An unexpected lithe half-turn, his corkscrew
torsion back and around to lock gazes,
the vibe that jolts us awake just as surprising—
so . . . obstinate? so shaken—where some four
or five in-rushing attitudes competed.

I wondered if any but a wrestler's waist
and neck could helix up to exhibit
the blush, the cool resilience of a face
still damp from a hot shower, and maintain
our stable dovetailed tempo further down.

Espresso ringlets tangled over blue-green
eyes bracketed to one side like a film star,
jaw clenching, and no routine f-word needed
to convey the ache, the angry exultation
that can't help being selfish when it feels good.

OK, my chuckle's too much of a gloat,
so you lean back for a snog that shuts me up,
teamwork teasing the brink until one vaulter
arcs and plunges earthward .... Left behind,
all right, but no complaints from this postponer.

As both sides of our bodied Mobius
strip become each other, you'll soon be seeing
me make my half-turn, trusting to meet your gaze.

<u>In Half-Light</u>

its source the twilit window. Bedcovers an hour
ago thrown off coil in linen spirals on the floor.

Against the horizon, an outline, a solemnity,
a monument built during the last century.

Your belly, where my left hand, sensing the heartbeat,
rests on small damp curls, a track that leads

farther down to the shadowy epicenter,
its odd, ungainly, stunning generator,

love's least describable incarnation.
Terrain surveyed almost without volition,

in half-light, in a breathless aftermath deeper
even than the undersea drama that overtakes people

in sleep. Times like this used to cause anxiety,
but not now. Instead, an onflow of energy,

the outlook released when we shed a worn-out disguise,
or hear the live voice sounding, after someone dies.

Pam Crow

<u>Here</u>

How can one woman's skin hold so much light?
When my mouth brushes across the silken
desert of your belly, blossoms ignite
copper sparks on my tongue, darken
in certain curves to caramel. You invite
me deeper, where I can feel you open,
sense the heat adobe holds nearing night.

I sing of apricot and brass. Hidden
coals glow sienna, almost out of sight,
stoked by my hands and breath, by my brazen
heart which flickers in this landscape despite
those who hiss I should not touch a woman
here, and here. Yes. Pull down the stars tonight.

Hike to Frog Pond

Our daughter dances through the tall grass,
singing "Frogs no bite, no bite."
A plastic pitcher swings from her hand.
"One Mommy, two Mommies,"
she counts us across the field.

Wind fills out eyes and ears,
pushing breath back into us.
Danger is random here. The coiled
rattler in our path last summer,
jagged cliffs below our trail,
single out no one. This is different
from laws we live and dream,
fear built thick and angled, shutting
out light, naming us unfit, unnatural.

The sudden hush of forest slows
our steps. We reach to stroke
plush moss greening on trees,
listen for the fairies whose homes
our daughter finds between
the roots of trees, in hollow stumps.
Stopping short, we see the pond
has disappeared in summer's heat.

The earth is cracked and brown,
but hidden in a crease we find
a tree frog, no bigger than my
thumbnail. The more we look,
the more we see them—leaf green,
speckled and striped. One rides
a horse on my daughter's shirt,
one hops from knuckle to shoe.
We don't dare step.

Nothing has stopped them--
not the sun beating down, nor

that clearcut on the hill above.
As we head toward home we hear
their random croaking, persisting
through the story of evening.

<u>Crossing the Border</u>

They might ask you who your mother is, I said
some questions should be simple: how old are you?
what color is this?
my mother never knew her birth date
made up whatever suited her
grew younger each year, and her auntie said
the ocean around Rhodes was the color of her brother's eyes,
changing from green to gray to blue, blue, blue,
her brother who didn't leave on the ship to America
but crossed borders on a train headed to Germany.

The line of cars started and stopped.
We were headed through the Peace Arch to Canada,
having been married twice: once illegally, once in the nineties
when after a few months the county sent back our check, our marriage
certificate stamped CANCELLED in red ink
                Audre Lorde wrote: who said it was simple?

Say Gaby is your mother, I said, it will just make things easier

       in the back seat, strewn with Goldfish crackers,
       coloring books, Zoe hummed to herself and kicked the driver's
       seat.
Isaac, thumb in mouth, gazed from his booster chair out into the park,
Children of a Common Mother written on this side of the arch.
       Isaac, named for his grandfather, one of the Shanghai Jews,
       whose wife
       standing in line on Ellis Island pulled down long sleeves over
       her eczema-scarred arms,
prayed she would not be turned away.

Son, said the border guard when he put his face, his mirrored
sunglasses
through the driver's window, is one of these ladies your mother?
                Marilyn Hacker wrote: Who gets to
                choose what battle

takes her down?

Both of them, Isaac said, a generous man gave them sperm and then they made me up.

We have to take ourselves seriously or
die, wrote Adrienne Rich

OK said the border guard, and are you traveling to Canada for business or pleasure? Pleasure, we all said at once, and we drove on.

Lisa Dordal

<u>Sixth Grade</u>

Under a warm June sun during the break
between Social Studies and Language Arts,

they married us off. Our bodies surrounded
on the cracked pavement of our schoolyard

by friends, classmates, then
by something larger, sovereign and invisible.

Bruce in wide jeans, a pink Oxford button-down,
and brown tie-ups so shiny you could see birds

in the patches of sky they reflected. Everything
about him beautiful. Me, in a short purple dress

and soda-orange sneakers that the older sister
of my best friend told me *had to go*.

A boy named Peter officiated, spoke the words
that blended us together. The same boy

who told me there were two types
of women: that I was the kind men married,

not the kind men used for practicing
(what they never wanted to perfect).

Even in the race-sore seventies
on Chicago's South Side, no one minded

this one rupture, this one tear in the
taut dictates of order: that he was black

and I was white. But they wouldn't tolerate
our queerness. The clang of missed baskets—

other kids shooting hoops—was our music.
That, and the cursing that always followed.

The Lies That Save Us

Driving through Georgia,
we lie like Abraham.
Are you sisters?, people ask.
Yes, we answer. *Twins, even.*
Though we are dressed similarly
in broad-brimmed hats,
long-sleeved shirts and tan pants
tucked into thick white socks
(it being tick season and all)—
we look nothing alike.
Thought so, people say,
as if they have figured out
some secret code. We smile back,
knowing the power of things unseen:
atoms, quarks, and auras
and all the love that lies between.
Kissing energy, we call it.
But all they can see is
something.

Robert Fleming

<u>Stonewall Heels</u>

Dressed as a man, I'm taller,
    than a woman,
but wearing heels,
    I'm so much taller,
and that matters.

What hurts more?
    My soul against a shoe slope
        no my calve,
    no beaten with a club.
Officers, so hot in porn,
    but at Stonewall,
        fist after fist,
            and club after club,
                and no lube,
            hitting my back and my face,
                not even 1 slap
            on my butt.

At Stonewall, a heel
        became more
        than a shoe.
Drag queens, so fierce on the runway,
    but at Stonewall,
        no after no,
        and heel after heel,
    first catapulting heels,
        then holding a strap
and lashing the officers,
    until my heels and mascara were
        blood.

Now, I walk with a walker,
    and wear flats – 2 inches or less,

when I walk no more,
    I will be ashed
        with my Stonewall heels.

55

<u>Mile High High Heels</u>

High Heels don't hurt in space
but on earth,
       after 15 minutes,
mine do.

<u>Gay Resume</u>

Anal sex pains you,
Can~~not~~ fight in a war,
Sperm stains you,
Political change a bore,
Marriages are ~~not~~ lawful,
Commitments break,
Shallow men awful,
Might as well be straight.

<u>Farewell My Stonewall</u>

On the street, i'll look like a man,
        no-one will know,
                i'm a drag in a bag.
Like a scout, a drag's prepared-
        for trouble.
            I'm wearing,
                knuckles, under my gloves,
                        and know Mary's number,
                for bail.
At the club, with a double snap,
        i'll be a queen.
            In wig,
                on the stage,
                        under the discoball,
                                i'll get the attention
                I deserve.
At closing, i'll de-makeup
        and pray, on the streets,
                no-one will notice me.

Now, what's a drag to do?
            with mainstreaming?
            runway down the street
                in heels and wig,
nobody stares.
no more running
        from the streetlight.
on the streets,
        can't get an officer beating,
        wheres a drag to go?
for a good beating?
Trans have so many rights-
        those heels are gone,
                forever.

Bitter Queen

Let me lick your heels.
Give me abuse.
Step on me with spikes
Make me feel used.
Dominate me.
Your illusions are your charm.
I can't stay away from you.
Heal me with harm.

Chorus:

    Bitter Queen you are so mean.
    Your history burned your self-esteem.
    Watch you work a man.
    Watch you take him down.
    I want to be that man.
    Make me drown
    I can't stay away from you.
    Bitter Queen you are my need.

Your heart brake makes me laugh.
Your doom is a death row chair.
Your words are weapons.
You are the party.
You've repeated the mistakes again and again.
You've placed your heart in prison.
Your vow is never again.
You're closed to loving me.

(Chorus)

Bridge:

    All I have is your game.
    I want more from you.
    Put away pain.
    Do you want something real?

Stop being a bitch.
I see a girl I can love in you.
Do you have a heart to risk?
Take off your heels.

(Chorus)

Donna Fleischer

<u>Harvest Moon Folk Lyric</u>

the eucharist forced
down my throat at six
stuck to my palette gagging me because it was
so big

my own Jewish blood
kept secret until I was 16 when I cared only for
music, poetry, Hinduism, girls

years later there's nothing
between me and the harvest moon —

we make funny faces at
one another, sing songs, and
share the names of women we love

Charlotte Forrester

<u>Man Up</u>

Where were you,
When a group of drunken men
Pushed me against the fence
And poured beer on my head?
"Here's some beer, you sissy!"
All them cackled like hyenas.
I reached out for your hand
But you turned away from me,
"Sorry, you brought this on yourself.
You made the decision to get drunk
And dress in scantily clad clothing.
You keep misrepresenting yourself,
You're lucky you're not dead."
Oh, how I wished died then.
I cried
And you had the gall to tell me,
"Man up! You have balls! Stop crying! Stand up for yourself! Fight
back!"
How could have I fought back
With both arms being pressed against the fence
My clothes being teared off?
My body and existence outed for the whole world to see
Against my will
They laugh at my degradation.
Gawking at my exposed body with horrified curiosity;
"Nice bitch tits! Especially for a weirdo with a dinky wink!"
Despite my tears and scars,
You kept insisting that it was my fault
And that I'm on my own.

Queen of the Underground

She was the sweetest little thing to come from the Island.
Her eyes sparkled like diamonds in champagne.
Like her lips, her words sparked like orange marmalade laced with habanero.
Sweet at first, but left a slow burn later.

That was her style,
Toxic, yet intoxicating.
I knew she was irresponsible
But there's no denying that she was irresistible.

She boozed with the beaus,
She floozed with the lads
She used all she could
She lost all she had.
Sure, she'd done bad.
She was glad,
To say the least.

She was a mighty lady
With a lot of sass.
And while she was crass,
She could cast some wicked shade.
All hail to the Queen of the Underground.

<u>The Devil Lady</u>

I don't know who said it, but it was once claimed that, "there is no greater sin than being a woman."
We are damned if we do
We are damned if we don't
It is indeed the most bitter of catch 22's.
For there is no greater sin than being a woman.
Especially when she has balls.
In this wicked world,
There is no greater devil than a ballsy woman.
And if the Pope says so,
Then I am a devil lady.
I'll spread my wings
And shriek like a harpy out of hell
For all the devil ladies in the world.

Tara Fraser

<u>Fire Heart</u>

Tonight, my fire heart sings,
Its voice echoing
Off the walls and
Against the floors
Whom are dressed,
In sweet soda water and
Yesterday's gin.
Neon light skitters over tables,
Adds coloured halos
To the sweet ones,
Electrifies the good ol' bois,
As they pulse to the beat.
I search the room for Anna,
Find her with another,
Their lips, softly feeding, on silent agreements,
Bleeding their heat,
in the back-booth's seat.
Upstairs,
The faded moon blinks
Highlights all our secrets
While
In the bar down below
Me and the Silverfox
Trade wishes
My hand rests on her rugged shoulder,
As her smile drips down
Finds home between my thighs.
"I like this, keep it on" she whispers
Hands stretched over my dress
Like a thick jacket that
Memorizes each curve

From somewhere far away,
A low murmur of cars
buzz over the silver fences
And past concrete cabins
And unlit lanterns
She memorizes each curve
Tonight, my fire heart sings.

Eddy Funkhouser

<u>young LGBTQ lives</u>

people struggle when telling stories about me in the past tense
when they talk about my childhood
my "girlhood"
they stumble over my name
my pronouns

if I had a nickel for every time
I heard "when
she was a little girl"
sometimes followed by
"that was your name back then
I don't get what you're so upset about"
or sometimes followed by
"I'm so sorry I support trans people I support you please forgive me"
I'd be able to donate a lot more to The Trevor Project

The Trevor Project is dedicated to saving
young LGBTQ lives
a suicide hotline for our youth

I wonder what fraction of those
young LGBTQ lives
now closeted
will grow up to be out
with a new name new pronouns
and people who cannot tell stories about them

I came out when I was twenty
people don't talk about before that
it's too hard for them to mince around my name my pronouns
my entire childhood and adolescence
erased
everywhere except my own memory

most of those stories aren't worth telling
or if they are
only as cautionary tales or
as macabre narratives proffered as currency
entry into hushed conversations
marginalized people sharing trauma

I wonder if my
young LGBTQ life
would have not had enough
substance of misery to buy into those
exchanges of spoken tragedy
if someone else had enough nickels to donate to The Trevor Project
so they could save my
young LGBTQ life
so I didn't have to work so damn hard to
save my own

Davidson Garrett

<u>Blasted Out of Dixie</u>

My final farewell conjures darkness,
passionate teardrops of freezing rain
fall from a sky sobbing golf-ball hail
surprising the slumbering New South,
blanketing weary magnolias with snow,
turning its fertile land into thick ice.

A twelve-hundred-mile escape on ice
ahead, my car flees in winter darkness
a town buried under glacial snowdrifts—
more accustomed to gentle spring rain
and lyrical breezes singing southerly,
than for precision bombing by hard hail.

The perilous odyssey brings *Hail
Mary*s to the lips—as the blue auto Ice
Capades on the slippery highway, south
of the river that evokes gothic darkness—
while the white night vies for a regal reign,
battling the moonlight with clouded snow.

Vicksburg surrenders to the Snow
Queen, lazy tongues declare—*hail
has frozen over*, raging gods rain
wrath with sharp arrows of dry ice
to punish prejudice toward skin of darkness
in this frigid heart of the Bible Belt South.

Recollections of a boyhood in the South
flood a tired mind, recalling snow
jobs by cross-burning fools of darkness
wearing hooded choir robes—hailing
Satan as they packed black bodies on ice—
washing the blood away with dirty rain.

On the road a last time, nostalgia rains
on the brain, in this timeless, surreal, South.
Suddenly, a service station rest for iced
Coke, to numb my body cold as snow—
never to forget the cold trajectory—of the hail
of *KILL HOMOS*—blasting me out of darkness.

Rain, snow, hail, ice,
a tempest only befits my Southern goodbye—
as I escape the darkness of hate.

The Bathhouse: A Sestina in B-Natural

Towels wrapped around waists of hard torsos,
half-nude men swagger through darkened halls
concealing their prized penises—
seeking relief for sexual frustration
interwoven with repressed guilt & fears
while HIV lurks, threatening the game.

Strangers cruise in a sensuous game,
roaming eyes gaze at buffed torsos—
steroid-pumped torsos full of queer fears
gathering in a maze of narrow halls
scented by poppers. Succor for frustration
while couples pair-off to worship penises

in a market place stocked with penises
devoid of rules dictating the game.
An escape for closeted frustrations
with plenty of big rippled torsos
massed safely together in eerie halls
retreating from deep-rooted boyhood fears.

Years of amplified homophobic fears
by preachers damning acts of penises
echo like screaming ghosts in steamy halls
haunting players in this erotic game
as smug narcissists lure torsos
begging a quick-fix for carnal frustrations.

Midnight approaches, pent-up frustrations
are drugged by crystal & coke; ever fearful
arms enfold around perspiring torsos
as lucky mouths suck erect penises
inside cubicles. Scoring in the game—
exploding orgasms rumble the halls.

At dawn, the anonymous halls
greet a fresh batch of homos—frustrated,
allowing a new team for the sex game
to mollify suppressed religious fears.
Roving hands jerk agreeable penises
dangling from the groins of tender torsos.

Biblical fears of penises
created this torso-hunting game
in grim halls pacifying lifelong frustrations.

<u>Death in Harlem Hospital with Straussian Overtones: 1986</u>

No operatic good-bye
    the morning you died
of AIDS; only a sigh

of grief. I then cried
    taxiing home,
a long autumnal ride

past the hidden dome
    of the cathedral. My
brain began its comb

for a tidy reply
    to white-lie amend
& demystify

death. Couldn't pretend
    with an Elektra-mind—
but did violently rend

all excuses designed
    to disguise. Your cold
dead corpse—reclined

in a morgue of mold
    alone & battered—
your Queens' mother I told,

was shattered.

In Memory of Richard Jurgis

Tova Green

<u>Freedom Summer, August, 1963</u>

"You're asking for trouble," she told us.
"Whites and Colored don't mix here."

We were two white girls, college students,
knocking on doors in a black neighborhood

in Greensboro, North Carolina, registering people
to vote. Some doors opened, some didn't.

We got lost on our way back to the Baptist church
that sheltered us and twenty other black and white students

and stopped to rest in a park. The long-armed
leafy branches shaded us from the heat,

protected us from being seen. The kiss
took us by surprise. Later we teased one another

about who started it, how our sweaty bodies
moved closer, how we leaned towards one another.

I stroked Nora's hair – or did she put her arm
around my shoulder? Or did our cheeks touch,

our heads turn, making the kiss inevitable?
That kiss was sweet and long, interrupted

by the shouts of children coming to play ball
in the park. We slowly rose, brushing

grass off our skirts and found our way back
to the church. A few nights later

all twenty-two of us boarded a chartered bus
bound for Washington, DC. A police car

escorted us out of Greensboro. Nora and I
shared a single seat and kissed in the dark.

We woke up in Washington to the voices of children
singing freedom songs.

<u>Liberty</u>

My breasts press
against her broad back.
My legs nestle
behind her strong hips.
My arms encircle
her waist.
She steps on the gas.
We pass bicycles,
buses, blurs
of buildings,
greens of trees
as we speed
through the streets
of Berlin,

I'm here
for the ride,
for the joy
of the ride
a Jew
born in the 40's
on a blue scooter
named Liberty
in a city
where once
I would have been
erased.

Sean Hanrahan

Dolmen Man

I phoenixed myself out
of the ashes of a
greater or lesser self
risen from the stray half
life of cooling embers
banked by debasing love
Mediterranean
and rare but valueless
grooving to a house beat
subterranean and
a sudden death too left
to quantify death on
a chilly Tanqueray
rock death on a swizzle
stick cherry rotting quick
under a fluorescent
sun queens willow over
a jukebox Judy or
Barbra clarion call
mechanized yet tuneful
AIDS costs a quarter is
stopped for a buck and straight
concern is just a two
dollar bill but we're not
oppressed the fronting
hurts more than the comments
do and they ain't worth shit
not repressed enough for
some but scorned enough for
others sweetly sipping
amaretto out of
a stiletto combing
through ends of a lace front
wig searching for meaning

in the soft sweat smoke smell
airing grievances of the
misbegotten and the
late forgotten in the
politics a tremble
of an ever red fan
real estate on a quilt
and the reverb from a
karaoke song life
slumped trapezoidal on
a barstool cradled by
poems from a diva
blessed by barbiturates
crowned by fairies trailing
lights only we can own

<u>Groom on a Cake</u>

I've decided to take
the plunge off the end of
this cake I am moored in
fondant disinterested
minds conferred whether to
bestow humanity
on us and devised some
greeting card prose legal
meaning we still can't get
married by a preacher
only Cinderella's
fairy godmother with
all the legal standing
such a union implies

We are entitled to
the jokey Bud Lite cans
hitched to Mississippi
mud truck flaps if we crash
the doctors can refuse
us life because of our
rings we both grow dizzy
from the political
whirligig rides that make
us puke cotton candy
on our designer clothes

Separated from my
groom on the vanilla
expanse he loosens his
collar as fiery
judgmental eyes melt him
to a waxen puddle
purple flower submerged
in a supposed sin

I will jump oh I will
survive and I will keep
the wilted boutonniere
in anger for remembrance
our assimilation
a miscalculation

Morals Clause

The stalwart Hollywood tall construction
imploded—a saturated tan salon peach fade
to wan white. Lanky death throes of a
made-to-order star on a fainting couch
once used for casting the role of the Invisible
Flame. Pool boys divvy up straight exchanged
wealth before the corpse draws cold. Shudders
from a fever dream of studio sets and beautiful
blondes. Tabloid hungry boyfriends bottle
beefcake night sweat into perfume to spritz to the
tune of Judy and sell to the orgiastic shutter clicks of
paparazzi glee. Size thirteens kick the slick sheets
of a former giant who loomed over the titles of
melodramas and sex romps where the gay acted
straight acted gay sporting Doris Day's virginal nighties
to show up the sacrificial effete comic relief—the submissive
to Hays-approved dominance. Acres of *Photoplay*
spreads dedicated to bearded ladies. Publicity puff
pieces with the lazy authority of burgers and Scotch
consumed over a prolonged masculine Sunday. He
once left his Turin blurry face on a dinette napkin
now secreted in a camphor drawer—safe for future
profiteering. When he was playing stud poker with John Wayne,
could he have imagined he would become an emaciated,
gnarled saguaro without bloom? Cradled by Our Lady
of AIDS who did more than anyone since jewelers
could have cut glass on the hard brittle white Reaganite
unconcern. Did the Astrologer to the Stars divine his
death in her zodiacal zigzags or Lipton tea leaves or just
through reading the *Enquirer*? Box office power kept the butch
wrangler from inky *Confidential* destruction. His life a commodity.
His death a commodity. Humanity just a celluloid commodity.
Six-foot-four hunk of virility not Gibraltar Rock at all but clay.
Ashes may have drifted from LA to his Hudson River namesake.
Christened by Wilson. Rejected by Christ. He rose again in
Dynasty reruns. He's now entombed in the rubble of forgotten

contractual Universal roles shown to a shrinking audience,
but all we can see
is that familiar mid-eighties haggard, hallowed face of gay martyrdom.

82

Phasers Set to Stun

We gays don't figure in
adolescent sex dreams
of bedding tri-boobed
blue beauties or conquering
hostile galaxies with verve.

We're just sexless pariahs
or paternal figures banished
to forgotten planets unvisited
except for the off-chance
heroes seek digestible maxims.

Contractually forced to mentor
whiny boys weapon training
them to be real men rewarded
with loveless death killed off
in the first episode.

Apparently gays cannot survive
space escape pods mysteriously
tampered with someone must
go down with the spaceship
we were never allowed to design.

Lesbians fare no better written
off to make room for straight
women the plot lifted from
second wave feminism in the
future heteronormativity is the spice.

Gaffe tape chaffing Carrie's breasts
like the tug from a drag queen's sack
clad in draped virginity and cinnamon
rolls flirting with the rogue dull
kink locked in an incestuous kiss.

We should just storm trooper this studio
set with phasers set to stun no time
to wait for inclusion let's wage
Battlestar Galactica beam ourselves
up no one is doing it for us.

Stop drop and vogue Shatner style
the awkward pauses not found in
Shakespeare wield lightsabers in
more vibrant colors it's outer space
why are we still chained to earth?

<u>Straight Jacket</u>

You need shoulders wider
than your hips but your hips
can't swish you need a wide
crotch walk not a prance or
a mince you need a deep
bass voice drop the lisp the
overly animated pitch
put this jacket on so
the shoulders slope let it
manfully define you
in the hope you present
less fairy more Mitch we'll
tighten it for safety
and straighten you for life
feel the lining of it
you'll be pining for it
every last stitch and twitch.

Hannah Harris

<u>Futch (as a broken hand mirror)</u>

is
loose pants,
dyke walk, short nails
(pop off the first two three acrylics),
police my wide hips fat ass booty short sport bra
fire hazard. dichotomies denim & Birkenstock bible belt
butch, lipstick on the blunt bitch. God wears boot-cut jeans & a
bicep tattoo, their heart is a blindfold. Futch is the sailor knot. Show
me your scars. Futch is a fumble in the dark. a gnarled souvenir fridge
magnet, an alphabet soup orgy. a blade swimming across a fleshen
lake.
waveless. a fat lip, fingers stitched, bitten. Futch is the mole on my
right
ass cheek. a fishnet facemask, robbing REI in millennial pink hair
ribbons.
fuzzy handcuffs and undercuts. Futch is an accidental burp, a lady in
waiting.
Futch is a new history, voices tangled in an ugly missionary position.
Futch, the synthesis of femme and butch, is a yin yang yard sale.
birdbones covered in motor oil. a cuffed denim ballroom
dancer, Futch is a mid-field grassangel.
neutral as a bandana gas mask.
Futch is a language
scattered & arced
into multitudes,
a sparkling
world
we built
large
enough
to
contain
us.

Sandra de Helen

<u>Tuxedo and Gown (Beautiful)</u>

We were beautiful the day
we went to the prom. The
gay and lesbian prom took
place on June 15, 1984. You
rented a tux, I bought a
vintage gown and let out the
seams. We both had the
loose curls of romance, and
the pink bloom of youth.
Your photographer friend
came to the house and
took professional shots of
you, me, us, my cat, our
flowers, piano, and the
sun streaming in the windows.
You were slim, handsome
in your white shirt, black
tux, cummerbund and tie, I
was voluptuous and beaming
in shell pink tulle, white lace,
rose pink taffeta with satin
undergarments that made
seductive music when I walked.
We look like newlyweds in
that stack of photographs.
There is a shot of our hands
in white-gold filigree rings with
expensive stones, holding hands,
though we were never wed,
only divorced after nineteen
years. On prom day we
were beautiful.

<u>Tarantism, n. an extreme impulse to dance</u>

Our first Halloween. You dressed as a
sailor, and I was your slutty wench. I wore
heels, and a black dress with a slit up to
here. Here where you can feel my heart
beating for you, but later, later. The
Dyke Tones are singing, and I have an
uncontrollable urge to dance, to feel
your strong arms around me, to lay
my head on your shoulder, to press
my leg between yours in a slow dance
meant to lead to ... later. Later, when
the dykes are no longer playing our
song, when the women are ready to
stagger out into the street in a throng.
Later when you take me home and oh
so slowly remove the dress, the torn
stockings, the fear from my heart that
you might not be the one.

<u>Becoming Lesbian 1977 Version</u>

Wearing makeup is as unnecessary as
painting crickets. Makeup is a tool of
the patriarchy. If you paint your face

wear dresses, wear your hair long,
put on soft sweaters, silky blouses,
you are doing it to attract men and

you aren't a real lesbian. Anne will
cut your hair. I'll take you to the thrift
store for jeans and flannel shirts. You

have to get rid of those skirts and
heels, dresses, coats, hats, gloves,
stockings, slips, nightgowns, and

lingerie. You need cotton underwear
and socks. Boots. You can have a
pair of cotton Mary Janes from China

for summer. (Thank Goddess! One
femme item allowed!) I sure hope
this transformation is worth it!

<u>In The Dark</u>

Everything you ever say
in the dark I say in
the daylight but that
sends you scurrying
like a silverfish
for your moldy book
or a thick new tome
never willing to
face the poetics
of the night in the
light of the day.
Under the moon or
the starless velvet
skies I hear your
silken or hoarse
whispers of desire
flattering phrases
describing my limbs
my skin, my moist
proof of yearning
for your touch. When
I am moved to sing
these same psalms
in the morning rays
to you, to your
neck, your shoulders,
your smell, that
place you called
your bathing suit
area when we were
children together…
you need to read
and I am left to
sing my aria to
the window above the
sink as I make our
morning tea.

Today's the Day

This is the day I go for it. Full out, full
stop, no holding back. Plan A all the
way. I'm straightening my shoulders,
pulling in my chin, leading with my
attitude.

I'm not asking for a favor, not pleading
for a cause. I'm telling them what is
what, and what that is is what I want.
I want full recognition, full rights under
the constitution, full benefits under all
laws, I demand to be seen, heard, and
felt. This is no dream where when I
punch them, it's like a hankie wafting in
a breeze. No. This is real life where a
fist landing on a body hurts both
parties, maybe not equally. But it
gives pain.

They have to listen. They have to
look into my eyes, my heart, my
soul, and see themselves looking
back, reflected as the same person
the same soul as me.

They have to. It's the only way.
I have no backup plan.

Scott Hightower

<u>The Anvil</u>

(500 W. 14 Street, beneath The Strand
Hotel, Dalamater Square, NYC)

The Anvil is an underground
late night (afterhours) claimed
space: meat, down and dirty;
black t-shirts and denim jeans.
"Gentlemen, WATCH
YOUR WALLETS!" blasts
every fifteen minutes from Patrick,
keeper of the infamous backroom.

Earsplitting, mesmerizing disco beats
pump over projections.

Tripping, I lead my callow
lover… and we watch

jaded bar dancers in lace-up boots
and torn and stretched-out tighty whities
sometimes reach up for the support
of crude single, rope trapezes,
Then other features;
dancers with enormous metallic
fans, a naked man
with flame-engulfed hands
exploring his own crevices.

After hours, we make our way
back up the stairs and roll out—
reaching for our shades—
into bright,
sunlit Sunday
morning taxis.

The Mineshaft

(835 Washington St, Little W. 12 St.,
Oct. 8, 1976 – Nov. 7, 1985)

Dark. And grimy. Promiscuity
is celebrated. Nudity,
minimal, or fetish clothing
is encouraged:

NO DISCO DRAG or DRESSES
NO RUGBY SHIRTS, DESIGNER
        SWEATERS, or TUXEDOS
NO SUITS, TIES, DRESS PANTS
NO COLOGNES or PERFUMES

A "clothes" check is provided.

Recreational drug use
is far from rare.

Upstairs, there is a pool table,
Point of departure and return.

Downstairs, most men voluntarily
strip and slip into scenic
spotlighted fantasies made real:
cells, slings, or bathtubs
that other men might respond
to them. This—the theater
of access and humiliation,
affection and torture—
is where one flees the country
to escape prosecution.

*

Now ("the less-desirable elements
that prevented investment" having been
removed) the landscaping trees
of the Standard Biergarten
and the four
cheerful, striped umbrellas
of the Standard Hotel Grill
beckon from just across the way.

The Saint

The Saint slips away,
a closing blossom, a glossy
black 80s match book,

a majestic gay haunt,
similar in its own way
to the opulence of White's
ever-evolving Madison Square Garden.

Each week the spectacular
floor-through entrance walk
was glorious (one night,
thousands of tulips
along a yellow brick road);

no drinks, shiny bowls of fruit
fit for the gods; and late
into the morning
its upstairs dance floor
would ultimately bloom
open. Everything was flashy,
throb and pulse.

You moonlighted there
as an emergency medic.
I—*chocolate cake and ice cream*—
waited for you, tripped,
and danced my heart out.

<u>Riding Pillion</u>

Rachel (Richard) Humphreys, 1952-1990

In the sputtering era of someone else
claiming their success, three years
(somewhere between 1974 and 1978)
is not necessarily a long time.

"I make a better woman
than I do a man." Remember
the shimmering city
is a funny place. The ridiculous

insecurities and certitudes
of familiarity, affection,
and self-possession —
unlike the compromising

sleaze and corrupting rebellion
of glamour—do not melt away
in the mainstream. Your unclaimed
body is one of the many

that has been given
a utilitarian—
no fanfare—
burial on Hart Island.

<u>Philip's Song</u>

(In memoriam, Philip Stansbury)

The enormous opening robot bear
with hatch—the introducing prop--
containing Miley Cyrus is a promising beginning. But
the fantasy dance
of a little girl's independence
sadly becomes a jumble of movements
and gestures of rebellion and, then,
enmity, malice, and defiance.

By the final scene of "The Graduate,"
we all know Benjie is going to end up
in "Pasedena Plastics." Elaine,
full of regrets, will be staring
away, stunned by a martini. Both
should have taken a bit more
time and studied Mrs. Robinson.
She is the one most likely to befriend
and ending up hanging or running
with the fluid Karen Walker
of *Will and Grace*, or—better yet—
with the girls of *Absolutely Fabulous*.

Cyrus's bare tongue wags
to its rehearsed sexual pose,
her rock dilutes down
to a (cough cough)
commercial package deal.
Nothing really ripples.

Rather than "Girl Exhibits Her Way
To a New Stage of Maturity,"
what gets flaunted is hollow excess
and infantilism…. Achy breakie my heart.
All that promise… then, sadly, nothing

but blurred lines of mechanical display.

It's not the premiere of "The Rite of Spring,"
nor that this young woman lacks
talent; but legions of urbane women
--and a team of urbane man in
artful wigs, in a cloud of makeup,
and passing a hair brush—
have channeled ardent revelation.

Philip, my friend, told me
about his Louisiana parents
one night announcing that it was his
"Last Halloween going-about-in-costume!"

Naively, he squeezed into his little
sister's black velvet zip-up onesie:
hoodie, thumb holes, and footsies.
And playful young artist that he was,
he grabbed a ball of yarn ….

Later, he confessed nothing
had prepared him for all
the indiscrete attention
in men's eyes.
          "… Before the end
of the night, I grasped
that I could commandeer"

(and that he greatly preferred)
"—rather than some succumbing
cat, the more majestic
self-possessed
persona of Maleficent."

Walter Holland

<u>Kick Line</u>

Some queen formed a chorus line, delirious, silly, exuberantly mad,
faced the ire of the cops, who with their nightsticks shouted

for the frivolity to stop, those showy hijinks from some lisping
sissies, homeless boys and faggot queers in every shade of brown,

who lived in parks, or slept on streets and washed in men's room stalls.
So, these limp-wristed, mincing, prissy pervs pushed back against the blows

as onlookers—men who passed for men—fairies of the ivy leagues
with adman suits and ties, who lived lives in opulence and hid behind

their artful lies, who never bed the riffraff without a stash of cash—stared
at the rough trade and tranny trash that tore down the barricades and chased

the chasers down those hidden lanes, where pain and blackmail long
had reigned and love was never asked its name.

Sylvia Rivera at the Docks

In the final moment her vagrant hovel of torn plastic and
boxes battered by the harbor winds with leftover paper plates

and traces of canned food, was deemed a health nuisance, and
by order of Sanitation commanded to be taken down, demolished

that instant by the police. She staggered with haggard face and crazed
eyes, tear-strewn as she screamed some mad diatribe of expletives

and voiced her total disgust, walking in circles around the cold pier, no
longer in control, emaciated, sickly, well-past middle age, the City skyline

just behind: luxury high-rises with spiraling rents near homeless
shanty towns, and, knowing all the while of the cancer spreading

inside, the waves of untreated pain, totally defeated by the inequities
of her life, the hard-knocks-adolescence caused by her "aberrant" nature,

one more seedy street-person or trashy freak, to pick up, fuck, and kick out
of a limo, she sat down and cried. But, in the end for me, she will

always be that thin queen in disco pants with a flower tucked in her
hair, rouged lips, beaming with Puerto Rican pride, yelling into a mike

her memories of that night, the night Stonewall burned when she
had fought, one angry flaming Latina, now booed from the stage.

D. Scott Humphries

<u>Before the early days of the dying</u>

The black men all liked Billy. Something Billy said.
Something Billy did – his hot, dusky musk –
moths fluttered to his Dietrich,
from head to toe *auf Liebe eingestellt*,
that was our world, can't help it.

His fearful mother in Muncie hated when Billy, as a teen,
invited the black boys by to sun in the yard for all the town to see.
Billy became black, his destiny,

the way I became an honorary Jew.
A *mensch*, my Jewish men friends said,
because I knew the nuance of the word.

Then, educated gay white men first fell ill,
wasting away, lying in their own filth.
No one would enter their rooms.
Cold trays of hospital food left in the halls

until lesbians, no longer other, became caregiver
and friend. Until we created our own structures,
together stitched a quilt – threads of lives
drenched in blood, in semen and shit, turned
into a fabric, art. We had life by the balls.

Later came women, the poor, addicts
and accidents, contaminated needles on the beach,
in the water, even on the wards.

Who owns these stories, passed down now through gender,
race, along the margins and hospital halls?
Those gay white men are tired or gone. But not only white,
not even in the early days of the dying.

Billy knew, stripped bare in the darkness,
degrees on the wall, wallets in trousers balled on the floor:
we were all black,
or white as a blood cell when the sun hit us at noon.

The disease knew it too.

Bringing Billy Home (Numbers)

You died at 31, when I was 32.
In '98, I reached 40 for us both.
Now I am 60; you're dead 26 years –
nearly as long as you lived –
my age has since doubled.
San Diego '81 to '86, West Palm Beach '87 to '91,
10 good years if there was anything good
about the 80s. Most of the time I think
there wasn't: 51,337 deaths from '87 to '89,
you one of 28,569 in '91. Then there were
those 3 films: *Parting Glances, An Early Frost,
Longtime Companion,* difficult to watch,
available now free on YouTube. Once a year,
or twice, I watch those 3 films horribly,
religiously. In '94, I brought your ashes
from Florida to the New Jersey woods.
In '02, I went abroad for 14 years.
2 years ago, I returned, all along renting
those 3 movies, 1 at a time, then watching
them on YouTube – 3 films that so perfectly
capture a terrible time, they remind me of you,
more than your ashes, Jim's ashes, Don's ashes,
all ashes, you have survived in those 3 films online.

Do I miss you?
Do the math.

<u>Billy Says Goodbye to the 80s</u>

The first one, five minutes, yet you knew where you were:
Florida, home at the condo. After the second, I found you

sitting in CDs, trying to alphabetize, confused,
kitchen in shambles since you'd decided to toss

every product with sugar. Something had snapped.
The third, early November, Gloria couldn't lift you –

another day on the floor until I returned.
In the ER at St. Mary's, you said call my brothers

in Texas, my mom back in Muncie, tell them:
don't wait for Thanksgiving, they should come now.

At your hospital bed, you completed my thoughts
as I ended your sentences. Finally, I asked:

what memory meant the most, I needed to know –
the day we met in the Navy cleaning toilets together,

nights at the Top Deck down in the Gaslamp,
holding court in the weight room, me cruising the pool?

You said, yes, San Diego, but not at the baths. Balboa Park:
a group of gay sailors and some dykes playing Frisbee,

spread out, you almost over the hill, waving and screaming
throw it to me, here I am, pick me, why won't you throw it,

and when someone did, you ducked yelling *I can't.*
You cracked us all up as only you could, still makes me laugh for no
reason;

now there's no reason. Next day, semi-conscious
calling childhood names, mine not among them. Not that
it mattered. I had the Frisbee – at least the thought of the Frisbee.

Had I still had the real thing, I'd have cremated it with you

the following Monday, twenty-first of November, just before
turkey, before dressing, dessert, before your family drove home.

<u>Don prepares, 1992</u>

Rehab could not hold me –
back out blinded in uncertain night,
dark alleys beside bar-lit doors.
I cannot remember who or when,
the moment it happened.

My mother speaks to my doctors
as if the halt of each infection
must cure overall; as if I will walk away whole,
permanently recovered
from pneumonia, or in remission
as if this were something simple like cancer,
as if it didn't happen when I lived in Atlanta
riding men instead of bicycles,
as if I were that boy who would,
like her first marriage, last forever,
as if her current husband is my father,
as if she weren't divorced, remarried, and Catholic.
Purity exists not in what you do
but in how you frame or recall it.

My lesions lie beneath neck-line or rage
internally, strategically placed tattoos,
bright red hearts with a banner
reading "mother," a reminder we are
bound in undiscussed guilt.

Let her build false hope on rumor.
When I'm gone she'll say I'm gone
without saying I've died or why.
At the service, not a funeral,
she'll lay me to rest, not bury me,
though I will be in the ground
in that plot off Congress Avenue,
close to the Port of Palm Beach.
She'll be pleased to hear you visit
some lunch hours. You'll never

hear that from her. Take it from me,
though, somehow, you'll know.

Christopher (30 years on)

You were already half blind,
the day that I met you,
back porch at a party, avoiding
the others, joint after joint,
my doppelganger alone, never sharing –

they called you my grumpy
kid brother, though we weren't related.
We both had brown hair, thin frames, both
thirty, though my eyes are brown and
your eyes were green, mysterious green –
opaque. I've no idea why
knowing you became so important.
No idea why, once while out jogging,
I ran with my eyes closed, trying
to be you, descending to darkness.
I missed all the trees whirling past
but the last one, brushed it and tumbled
down into the creek bed, blue water
cold as the wind on my one trip to Iceland

and just as confusing. At a restaurant
in Reykjavik, I ordered the puffin:
half parrot, half penguin, expecting it
to taste just like chicken. It tasted of fish,
which is all that it eats.

I should have known that. And I should have
known your frown had a lot to do with
being disowned by your family or
having a lover, disowned by his family,
who died first and left you a large
pre-war West Side apartment. Fully blind,

the one time I came calling,
you could not see the shit stain
on your leg or pajamas, could not even

smell it by then, nor did you know
who I was, but you could still stand
in that tall, open doorway, you could
still hear, cocking your head
at the sound of my breath
or my shuffle of shoe as I moved
about during the visit. Satisfied,
you followed me into the kitchen
where I made us some tea.

It was hard being young,
then, hard being thirty,
especially since you
couldn't see thirty-one.

Randall Ivey

<u>Homosexuality in Dixie: A Queer Sonnet</u>

The black cloth cover of the Good Book
Makes a fine veil to hide what is most vital
In you: your queer heart.

"Go into your closets and pray,"
Christ admonished, and you obeyed
And have never left that closet since

But shout out of it invectives
Against your own kind
As a way of smothering

The gentle cacophony of desire
That plays in you night and day,
Lest someone espies what is obvious to us all.

"The only way to hide," wrote the gentleman,
Is never to have been born at all."*

*Martin Greif on Willa Cather in the *Gay Book of Days*

Collin Kelley

<u>First Gay Crush</u>

Dirk was the name of my first gay crush,
goddamn how I lusted after that nerdy fuck.
I was 15 almost 16 and he was 18 going on 19,
and I was the prom queen hot for college cock.
His mismatched clothes, ill-fitting jeans, dirty sneakers,
my queer eye for a sexually confused guy already razor sharp.
I was too young to know I had control,
that my aim was true and his was scattershot
from years of strict military parenting.

We would sit in his dorm room
listening to Nina Hagen records
and watching *Doctor Who* on PBS.
I let my hand stray to touch his thigh, rest there
until he flinched as if flicked by holy water.
My father thought Dirk and I were fucking
after he caught me on the phone at 1 a.m.
in the dark living room.
Oh, Daddy, if only.
He would never come out of the closet for me.

Last night, I dreamed I met Dirk again in a coffee shop.
I saw him through the window, dark hair falling over his eyes,
his perfect white teeth a beacon.
I was thin again, like those last two years of high school
when I starved myself better than any cheerleader,
wearing a black coat tight at the waist.
I slid into the booth next to him and he kissed me, unafraid.
When I woke, all I could think about was the night
I told him I was gay and had fallen in love with someone else.
He gripped the steering wheel and stared straight ahead,
driving us into oncoming headlights.
"What," he screamed. "What do you want me to do about it?"

<u>Spring Hill</u>

- Midtown Atlanta

Spring Street where it crosses 10th,
the funeral home corner,
where they handed Uncle Terry back
in a cardboard box ten years ago.
Reduced him,
made him fit in a ziplock bag,
made him volcano dust and bone chips.
AIDS made him Pompeii.

In a yellowed newspaper 1951,
the births and deaths side by side,
Terry's name appeared opposite
a photo of that same corner.
The white walls and gabled roof,
biding its time, unchanged
save for the mourners' faces
and the bodies of those beautiful boys.

One day, I'll be taken to that corner,
so I take a good, long look,
memorize each brick,
in case the soul is blind or refuses to hover,
or if death is only blackness and I am just ashes.

<u>Sex Machines</u>

Heavy equipment outside my house
peeking in every window, oversized
voyeurs with names like roadheader
pile driver, pipe layer, knuckleboom
bottom dump, bulldozer, backhoe

I've got my back against the cool wood
of the dresser playing hide and seek
while a cherry picker threatens
to take off the tissue paper roof
my skin teenage virgin electric

The idea of exposure and crush
my legs wrapped around unbending metal
sends a ramrod shiver up my spine
all those edges to navigate and climb
or to be lowered into the dirt and mangled

Oh, psycho sexual infantilism, oh, paraphilia
you had me at birth, when I was another
object, my homosexuality a deviation on par
with rapists, molesters and humiliation seekers
I take this one for the team, machinery lust

your wrecking ball doesn't scare me

<u>The Beat of Black Wings</u>

They said when you got here,
the whole thing started.
Who are you? What are you?
Where did you come from?
I think you're the cause of all this.
I think you're evil!

> *– Hysterical mother in diner from Alfred Hitchcock's*
> *The Birds, 1963*

Someone must always take the blame – flight attendants or government bureaucrats, for example – but in this case it happens to be a cool blonde, maybe too icy in mint green, trailed by rumors from across the sea, dancing naked in a fountain, causing a scene. Because if there's no culpability then the world will spin off its axis, rotated by millions of flapping wings.

It begins in the big city, but that's too obvious, so take the action north to Bodega Bay, the tranquility ripe for destruction, the "it can't happen here" placidness broken only by seagull cries, as they wheel and dive over the harbor. And then one attacks, draws blood. Melanie Daniels, the stranger in town, becomes patient zero.

Soon, the birds are massing outside the door, indiscriminately pecking away at schoolteachers and children, ruining birthday parties, upsetting casual lunches and commerce. They perch in the most unexpected places; wake up with morning wood, hazy about whether it's your wife or boyfriend next to you, and find beady eyes staring back ready to put the peck in pecker.

No one is safe, not even farmers, chain smoking schoolmarms or overbearing mothers with retinas stronger than any contraceptive. Handsome men who spend too much time in the city with hoods and ne'er-do-wells, come home with soiled underwear and reeking of jazz and liquor, are also in mortal danger.

Realization sets in far too late, not until the air is filled with murders of crows. They wait, patient jinxes, until you're lulled into a false sense of security then attack. In the end, Melanie is drawn to the bedroom, left wide-eyed and ravaged, and the townspeople will says she got what she deserved for bringing the scourge upon them. But the radio crackles with news, the beat of black wings all the way to San Francisco.

Alexis Kennedy

<u>Dandelion</u>

I may be bright with colors, but sometimes

I still feel like
        just another weed.

When I die, I hope to leave behind a legacy

and I will finally be able to
        spread my seeds.

I created my seeds, nourished them my whole life,

and have given them everything
        they might need.

With a little bit of fluff and the help of a breeze,

the sky will take control, and the
        wind will lead.

My brave little seeds will fly far and beyond,

to their new home where they have
        finally been freed.

<u>Thank you, Pillow</u>

I'm thankful for my pillow.
It holds my head up while I become so vulnerable
as to let myself sleep.
It absorbs my sweat and my tears when I'm
fighting to survive the nightmares.
It remains soft and comfortable as I lay in bed
preparing to fall asleep.
It survives through all of the bad nights so I can
wake up knowing I survived too.

Sur* Landfried

<u>Mother</u>

Oh mother
you pretend to love me
but you´re talking ´bout
my hair too short
my clothes too mannish
my behaviour too extreme.

Oh mother
you pretend to love me
but you´re always calling me
by my dead name
denying myself
telling a history full of lies.

Oh mother
you pretend to love me
but in every conversation with you
my voice begins to tremble
my knees start to shake
and I need so much strength to answer.

Oh mother
you pretend to love me
but after each dialogue with you
I have to forgive your ignorance
I have to find myself again
and my power to survive.

Oh mother
you pretend to love me
but I love myself.
So the best I could do
- for me -
is to leave you behind.

<u>Words</u>

Violent words spoken
violent words
out of your mouth
their mouths
lots of mouths.
Violent words
trembling my heart
melting my pride
killing parts and parts
of me.

Short times of doubt
about myself
are followed by rage
I stand up and shout:
I´m not the trouble
not the inability
neither the guilt
nor the failure.
Open your eyes
shut your mouth
and listen!
Listen and learn
to change your words
to make them
warm hearts
rise pride
and honor all beautiful
parts of anyone.

<u>Passion</u>

Your lips painted red with care
black lined eyes
glances deliberately used
your dress dark lace
caressing your body
voluptuous collarbones hidden
but still perceivable
adorned curves
staged with plenitude
- seductiveness in perfection -
you look at me
a little smile
pursing your lips
your head tilted
slightly to one side
your skin crinkling
hardly noticeable
I´m tantalized
you tantalize me
with wilful intention
and I, I can´t resist
I fall prey
to your femmeness
to your powerful
play of temptation
your embodiment
of queer femininity
sends me to passion.

Amy Lauren

<u>I Saw a Woman in a Man's Clothes</u>

i.

He announces to pews of clutched-breath college students
as I tug flannel sleeves over white trembling fingers.
A friend had invited me to church, wanting me
to try again, and her pastor's pitching a mission

trip to my hometown. I've skipped half-drunk
through Canal St., but never handing out Gospel tracts—
besides, a yat couldn't miss rows of churches imposing
on manicured lawns. Yet students sign up to swarm

my hometown, button-up boys and teacup dress girls
with three-chord Trinitarian harmonies to battle
jazz's polyphonic clamor tumbling down streets.
It's hard to praise God in 5/4 time, but I saw a woman

clutching her clarinet and tapping her foot, blue hair
shaved in a fade, sweaty button-up outlining her binder.
My breasts ached like overripe creole tomatoes, neck itched
and I slapped it for bugs, but only my ponytail touched it/,

claws digging skin even when I wipe off sweat. This pastor
describes women dressed as men and my body hurts
again as if the witch who spun my voodoo doll
stuck in her needles.

ii.

While not fishing dogs out the Mississippi
or rescuing kids wandering from their mama's grips
on Esplanade, cops swept streets of whiskey-breathed
women who stepped too far outside their bars.

A femme could grab a tube from her bra, swipe lipstick
on her lover's lips to save their skin: exactly three articles
of "women's clothes" required. Or a femme was too slow,
cops grabbing her butch by collared pinstripe.

iii.

When this pastor calls New Orleans a swamp,
he means evil. He's right marshes seep from asphalt,
backyards erupt in crawfish mounds we kick,
pint-sized hurricanes smashing homes. You can pour

cement, but bury Mother Nature and earth
throws up her coffin. Moss-draped cypress
trees wrap gangling arms from which I'd shrink
as a girl, what my brother called ghost trees.

Even guarded by levees, we still crane our ears
for snake's rattles. Even picket-fenced mansions
sink in their own weight as stormwater drainage
shoves down my whole city. What good's a mission

trip? You can step on cottonmouths,
shoot mother black bear in her den,
or skin alligators for your wife's purse
but can't yank us all from the bog's jaws.

iv.

Sometimes, I'd imagine myself lipstick-ready
and pearl-lined, Stormé DeLarverie brawling
with men who whistled at me. Or I might be
Stormé, crooning jazz standards in my bowtie.

In my girlhood, the sight was a cartoon
preachers scrawled to scare children,
never an image I could resurrect
in myself. But I saw her playing clarinet
that day, top hat and all, no caricature,

just sandalwood cologne lifting humid breezes,
gold pocket watch on her wrist,
thick eyebrows framing dark roux eyes.

Cops haven't locked up women in men's clothes
in decades; or, if it happens anywhere,
at least it's not New Orleans. That's what
this preacher means by "swamp": magic

crept out bars, bled into streets, judgment
washing away our homes yet too weak
to scrub us from our roots. Whatever I am,
it's part alligator hunted to extinction's edge,

crawling back to swallow your Gospel.

<u>Evangeline</u>

Today I learned he died when I was twelve years old, told he was dead
long before. Family stopped speaking to him, and secrets are secrets

in English or French. He'd died of AIDS, blood-lunged. Years of
hacking
seawater and tugboat smog taught him to cough through warning
signs.

Just like his niece, who stepped on a catfish fin, a hook Papa tweezed
out
with pruning fingertips. My mother at eleven, appendix burst

in her burning chest because Papa called her cries childish whines.
I heard his words for relations like mine, never-married boys

who died in a Sister's arms. As a girl, I slept in my sister's arms,
safe harbor in a tumultuous home. Or at school, deep water

where I feared sinking. When my teacher found out I was gay,
she told me I'd never be happy, slipped invitations to church

in my portfolio, Christian school let her pray in front of my class.
I'd lie to make her stop, junior high stuttering, breath paused

for verdicts to walk the plank. She'd talk of drowning in fiery lakes.
If voodoo coaxed up my uncle's ghost, I'd ask him about drowning.

As a sailor, he surely feared plunging in the Mississippi. Instead,
tuberculosis swept his lungs and doctors refused to treat him,

family sailing away when he called for help. But I'd chase him,
over the Gulf, pull him into my arms, blood thicker than hurricanes.

Invisible Femmes

Her hands, little ghosts,
linger past final breath,
signing crosses on my chest,
absolving my heart's sins.
If I inhale incense

from the priest's vessel
suspended on chained metal,
she burns charcoal swirling
in sanctuary mouths.

Diamond dangling
from my neck, disappearing
when light dances, her name
shimmers in candlelight.
Church bell cracks shape
her face, moonlight illumes

her stained-glass wrists,
blessing begging thanks
from my lips—reverse magic
that makes us visible to
each parishioner who dreamt
we'd disappear.

David Lewis-Peart

<u>To 'Those'</u>

To the uncle I never knew
He went, my aunty said, the way many of 'those' others did;
quietly.

Men whose names were whispered, if said at all.

H.I....stories offered as warning.

This, to those that said
To those who didn't.
To others who couldn't.

To the men living with and loving through
To those men like some of you, who saw value in teaching and talking
and not going quietly.
To past lovers and friends.
To current ones too.

To the more than a few that chose to school - shame was a shitty way
to stay safe

To those who kept me/we teachable; in spite of my ignorance, and our
arrogance

To those who believed in a day where things would be different
To those many who worked to make sure that different, got done.

For that boy; some future mothers son,
who will fuck and love undefined and not confined by death and
disease.

His future, our future, is owed,
to the quiet and not so quiet, those.

R. Zamora Linmark

<u>Split-Second Serenity</u>

This afternoon I read about the time
Tim was admitted to Ward G-9 for AIDS
complications. Former lovers,
magazine editors, and writers
with drag aliases also dropped by,
as themselves or as apparitions.
But every night, at around six,
his lover Chris arrived to coax Tim
into finishing his meal, weep in
Tim's embrace, until the last second
of visiting hours. Most time, though,
Tim was alone, building a poem
that wouldn't, couldn't, stop growing,
as if it had a memory of its own,
tricked itself into believing that
staying unfinished meant more
time to disappear—an inverted
Scheherazade, you could say,
except we all know remembering
is tied to forgetting and cruelty.

Suddenly, I forgot where in Tim's
unending poem—if he were already
buried by an avalanche of love
or comparing the size of death
with someone from Marseilles —but
everything around me grew calm,
a split-second serenity
that required full submission.
And I, powerless and superstitious
to such visitation, started weeping.
For the life of me, I couldn't stop,
because Jorge was suddenly back
in full drag regalia en route to Tour Eiffel

before training it south to Rome for
a surprise splash á la Anita Ekberg
at the Trevi fountain. He dragged
along a suitcase of cocktails, rubbing
alcohol, Betadine swabs, a Styrofoam
cooler for the bags of IV antibiotics
I once watched him inject through a PIC
line above his heart. Then Stephen
chimed in, said, "Let's happy hour.
Hula's in half hour. Will shower now."

His lover William, our girlfriend Lisa,
and I got there first, ordered the
Sunday special: highball glass of
piña colada garnished with pineapple
wedge and, for the sakura effect,
a floating pink parasol toothpick.
We waited the length of three slow
rounds, took turns speaking to Stephen's
answering machine, until worry
drove us speeding to his condo.
There, we found him, standing
and shivering under the shower
for God knows how long, in a daze,
recalling nothing, everything falling,
water after water after water.

(First published in www.hivhereandnow.com as part of the HIV Here
& Now Poetry Project.)

Timothy Liu

<u>Pilgrimage</u>

All four wheels
on our airport shuttle

blew out at once

but no one got hurt—
our only choice

was to wait for help

or set out on foot
until we finally

made it to that

place, pausing
before a threshold

where riots had

broken out as you
took my hand in

yours & whispered:

*Two condoms
are walking down*

the street and pass

*an infamous bar
when one turns to*

the other and says:

*Hey, you wanna
go in there*

and get shitfaced?

Rejoinder

To the man who downs
four Guinness pints

before he puts his arm

around my shoulder
and says, *Let me be clear:*

I'll never let you get in

my pants though faggots
keep trying, must be

something about me

they find irresistible!
I've only got this to say:

if you really want me

to suck you off that bad
with your four wheels up

in the air, you'll have to

try harder, a mattress
sliding off a flatbed truck

into five lanes of rubber

mayhem, your body
laid out on a stretcher

with a pretty bow tied

on top of your divine
tumescence while we do

our little sober dance—

<u>Safe Space</u>

You can forget about moving to Toronto.
Or disappearing into the Amazon.
Poisoned by mercury as you sift through heaps of discarded phones.
Not a cell tower in sight.
Nor messages on Grindr or Scruff.
The Rio Tambopata snaking around each muddy bend.
A lone child bathing among caimans, piranhas, electric eels
While the elders gather in their ceremonial huts.
Plantains, yucca root, boiled eggs.
The dogs and wolves in neighboring villages howling
As soon as the sun goes down.
The child goes down too
In a river so dark only those who have not been called
By absentee vote can actually see
Getting struck by a lightning bolt to the head
Is the only way out
Of mountains so tall even conquistadors under Cortez
Could not breathe such airs
And live.
Six kinds of potato the only thing that would get us through.

<u>A Stone's Throw Fifty Years Later</u>

He's quite serious
about his social media

curation—dick pics

and donkey punches
not part of the

narrative. Behind

the posed holiday
smiles and the fam all

touchy feely lies

the menace, the bottles
of oxy just outside

the frame—grandpa's

HO train set disassembled
and put away

in the crawl space

where nasty creepy crawlies
have at it, not enough

light down there

to illuminate the spots
of rust congregating where

childhood ends

and adulthood begins
to colonize the hand-held

devices masquerading

as stocking stuffers
we can't quite

afford—spider-cracked

touch-screen glass beyond
easy repair evidence

of class struggle

and shameful regress.
Sorry if I couldn't

help you locate any

egress—no service
and a low battery

inside my panic-room

dungeon, come in, let me
remove your wireless

Skull-Candy ear buds

to get you to focus
on something other than

your insipid playlists

that haven't given
anyone a boner

in years—all those fake

orgasmic selfies
no one really likes

or wants to comment on

stuffed so far down the wet
casements I don't know

where to begin, how to

undo the leather teddy
your grandma once wore

zipped-up in a mothballed

bag the size of Texas
if Louis Vuitton

were a freeze-dried twat

one can casually snack on
while reciting verses

no one has been willing

to commit to rote—
fuck memorable speech

and selling fruit rolls

or tissue packs
on an after-hours train

where eyes are glued

to their phones, unwilling
to acknowledge

a single mother

who claims her trans
daughters Destiny & Hope

are dropping dope beats—

Chip Livingston

<u>52 Hawks</u>

driving through muskogee, highway 62
is barbed wire. impossible not to mention
matthew shepard. not to mention orlando.

dusk silenced, we fuck in the vw
to prove something, we're alive at least,
and long enough to drain the car battery.

sleep then wake to a nightstick.
good luck, a cop's jumpstart west
from a dawn mourning too red. the hawk

must be a sign. you miss its flight, miss
the next one. there, i point. but you are reading
on your cell phone. obituaries. another raptor.

then a kind of rapture in the wish i make
aloud: a hawk to land on a fencepost. we begin
to count. one: you read stanley almodovar.

hawk two salutes: amanda alvear.
hawk three: oscar aracena-montero.
the hawks sentinel the road like honor

guards. 49 in six miles. they are something
we sing out names to. rudolfo. antonio.
darryl. angel. juan. luis. 49 hawks

and a morning full as a dance floor.
the 50th, a falcon, we call matthew
and quit our haunting inventory.

i metal the vw toward i-44
to flee the prairie purgatory. two birds on air,
there. you see and name us: not missing.

~ first published in *Kestral*

<u>Finding Love in Chelsea</u>

To the right of the porn star & just above the drag queen,
You go-go-boyed on roller skates, when
I saw your picture on the back of HX magazine.

As Rollerboy you made the backpage weekend SEEN,
Pointed out by a love-rich, ill-read friend,
To the right of the porn star & just above the drag queen.

Knowing better, I asked how old. He smiled & said 19,
Then added that you go for older men.
That put a different spin on your picture in the HX magazine.

So young & yet already deviating from the mean,
Your leather jock & harness touting S&M,
To the right of the porn star & just above the drag queen.

I got your number & we did the blind date scene.
I liked you even better in the skin.
That picture didn't do you justice in the back of HX magazine.

Six months later & we'd just passed Halloween.
My friend had ripped the page out once again.
I checked out the porn stars & marveled at the drag queens.
Then I saw our picture in the back of HX magazine.

~ first published in *Barrow Street*

Guzzling Hafiz

The gag was tight across his mouth
At first, to save his crying out his mouth

No way to thank his master's service then
But taking in whatever came about his mouth

His master's P.A.'ed prick would piss
Inside his ass without his mouth

Cock proven, he'd been slave traded
No owner ever had to doubt his mouth

This master had paraded him
On Folsom Street, had rented out his mouth

And while his ass was tendered only by his Sir
Sir touted any hairy dick to rout his mouth

They toured nasty pig events in Amsterdam
Had porn producers scout his mouth

Hafiz praised those stardust days of ludes
And taking loads until his Sir licked out his mouth

My Master Hafiz, I should say, who's leading me
And doesn't know where we would be today without his mouth

~ first published in *Bloom*

<u>June 26, 2015</u>

When you became my groom, we were both grooms.
In a room hallowed by justice, just us benedicted.
Does a first kiss in a graveyard foreshadow 'Till death?
Surprised by the Supreme Court's decision if not Il Papa's

Benediction in a room hallowed by justice. Just us
Professional grooms, tailor-made for TV interviews.
Were we surprised by the Supreme Court's historic decision?
What a wedding gift. Galvanized. Who chose the day?

Groomed by professionals, tailored, interviewed for TV news.
Old rings our fathers' heirlooms hammered new.
What wedding gifts. Galvanized. An historic day.
Family in front of family, which is as good as God.

And the rings our fathers' heirlooms hammered new.
When you became my groom, we were both grooms.
Family in front of family, which is as good as God.
Our first kiss in a graveyard. It foreshadowed justice.

~ first published in *Kestral*

Richard Loranger

<u>#we</u>

When I wake up queer,
it's like every other day.
Like every day since I came out of my mother.
I don't know what any of this means.
But I do know the rollercoaster,
the ins and outs of light,
the flickering,
the pounding beat,
the omniphonic symphony of cells.
I know my cells, my nerves,
my stink and hair, and I know
that someone called them queer.
Applied the term queer.
Maybe it was me. I. The
phenomenon referenced as I.
Or maybe it was everyone.
In any case, "queer" – a sound
with a history, from the German "quer" –
oblique, cross, adverse, perverse, deviant.
Oblique: slanted or sloping, asymmetrical,
indirect, evasive – I am most of these,
sometimes all when I include the latter two,
when in fact I need to shade my queerness
for the sake of safety, perceived or real.
Cross: I cross streets with my walk,
step after step, breath after breath,
I cross boundaries and proprieties,
word after word, breath after breath,
I cross my own queer shadow indirectly.
Adverse: I oppose intolerance, I face aggression
(or am faced by it), I turn toward ignorance, toward fists,
and I observe them, and sometimes I am afraid,
afraid to move, afraid to stay, but I let them know I am observing,
and I wait to be seen, for eyes to light, and sometimes I am struck.

Perverse: I am turned the wrong way
because somebody make the sound "wrong",
said I am twisted, bent; I turn away from the truly bent
whose nature has been torqued from human back to mammal,
I smell their fear, I turn away, I gather, I turn toward.
Deviant: I take the side roads, the small roads,
I range off-road, into the wilderness, into the wild,
far from nonsensical structures, laws and manners,
into the open space unshadowed by towers and norms
where civility and anarchy meet and caress and fuck.

Now that's queer.

That's queer because it defies the utterance of others, or of those who
other, and loves the utterance of those who we.
That's queer because it takes things as they are, as much as one can, it
allows where centuries of stone would otherwise staunch.
That's queer because it allows, because it lets the vine grow wild, the
thirsty drink, the body become and behave and be a new form, a new
shape stretching and writhing in its own splendor, its own light, its
own scent turning heads across the countryside to see what new thing
        has emerged.
That's queer because it allows the new, damns preconception, damns
presumption, curses definition for the infinite, lets the mind see what it
will, not what it wants, not what it expects but what it doesn't expect,
        what might be.
That's queer because it savors when propriety pulls back its chair,
folds its hands, and watches warily, wantonly, bewitched as queerness
        unfolds itself on the table.
That's queer because it smells good, because it feels right, and that's
        always okay.
That's queer because it has its own scent, knows its own scent,
because it knows its face, in whatever configuration, of whatever kind,
kindly, and surely, it is what it is.
That's queer because it knows what it is, even when struck. Especially
        when struck.
That's queer because you know what you are, I know what I am, we
know what we are, because you are what you are, I am what I am, we
are what we are, because you feel right, I feel right, we feel right.

That's queer because it feels right in my bed. It feels particular, specific, necessary, whole, ecstatic. Because it belongs. Because it feels normal, right, the most normal thing there is, entwined and drifting perfectly to sleep.

When I wake up queer, I wake up.
I wake up to normalcy.
I wake up to skin, to touch, to human scent, my own or another's
      or both.
I wake up to easy air. To my lungs accepting air with ease.
To delicious air. To acceptance.
I wake up to seeing and being seen.
I wake up to all the human shit we pull on each other – longing, confusion, presumption, jealousy, sadness, acceptance. Seeing and
      being seen.
I wake up to we, to being one with the species rather than outcast, I wake up to connection, to a sense of umbilicus.
I wake up to we, to the many inside me, to they that comprise me, to the kaleidoscopic whorl of being and sense and life. To the tourbillion
      of life.
I wake up to we, to the verb of we, to the act of we, to we as in to be as in to free as in to accept, to allow, to welcome.
I wake up to welcome, to the elusive welcome of being in the world, of moving forward, of inventing new forms of being, existence and
      purpose and joy.
I wake up to the elusive which is not elusive at all, despite what they say, because queer is not elusive, queer is here, queer is very here, queer is evolving, queer is thriving, queer is we.
Queer is normal because queer is everyone and everything, and everyone is queer because there is no normal. Normal is ideology. Normal is propaganda. Normal is queer.
Queer is every day, and every day is queer. Every night is queer. Every sleep is queer and every waking is queer.

When we wake, we queer. Like every other day.
I don't know what any of this means, because this isn't about meaning.
It's about being. It's about doing. It's about living.
So let us live, fiercely, softly, colorfully, darkly, queerly, as the need requires.

Let us be. Let us very be.
Let us do, and breathe, and do, and touch, and do, and rest, and do,
    and wake, and do.
Let us queer, as we are, as we can, as we want, as we will, as we must.
Let us we.

Sassafras Lowrey

<u>Hard Won Home</u>

We storm the streets
Spilling out from subway tunnels
Clown car piled fire escapes

Sequins and glitter
Glinting
Like that first thrown bottle
Smashed

Like the shards that barely missed me last week
You the week before

The streetlights cast shadows
Haunting
Of the
Hirstories
we should carry
Strapped next to our hearts into our boots
But are instead too often
Rusted glitter buried in sidewalk cracks

We're starved for this
Body slams body
Circuit parties
Festival sidelines
Desperate to feel
To connect
To believe
We're not
Alone

On Monday
We emerge from the rainbow haze

Hung-over
On the memory of
Belonging
On the feeling of
Connecting
It's never enough
And also everything we spent lifetimes
Not daring to dream of

Tell me about your first pride
And I'll show you mine
The stumble for breath
Backwards falling into buildings
The sunrise walk over the bridge
To watch the festival bloom
Dilated pupils taking in
More than dreams could conjure

Floats
Glitter
The roar of bikes

That day I did not wear three pieces of women's clothes
Boots
Jeans
Ace bandage
Boxers
Button-down
I did not know
Not long ago
This would have mattered

The plague has never ended
Cocktails are not cures
And I know more positive than not
So I assume
Until told otherwise

We hug when we meet
Chest to chest full body hugs
Pressing our hearts towards one another

Their fists were in the air that night
Heels and bottles gripped tight
Queens
Butches
Queer kids
Homeless

We never learned this in school
Taught ourselves in youth center back rooms
On library floors
Newsprint riot photo documented eyes
From the mouths of our lovers

Now we talk of it daily
Tattoo it into our skin
Wanting them to know
The hirstory they walk upon
The scars carried
Lives lost
For this moment to come to pass

The heart is the size of a fist
We're built to love and fight with the same ferocity
Always have been
We bring our love to the streets
And kiss away the road rash in hard won homes

Deirdre Maultsaid

<u>Nervy Endings, Nerve Ends, Ends</u>

Gender congeals,
A clammy Alzheimer belly slap.
Nerve ends swerve.
Every girl-jot freckle dissolves.

Escape to taste the confectionary sugar.
Oh, candy floss: bind me.
Show me the meaning of pink gossamer.
Unknot, unknow my nerves.

But, nothing is outside power,
before or after power.

Boyhood wanes.

Only the indigo sky,
Only the spiral inside the spiral of hushed voice stars
Is the fractal we need.

Love deep indigo.
Oh earth, oh sky!

Travel the fullness,
As we repeat,
Until we are too small
To identify.

(Know. Gender is like Alzheimer's.
But, let's go to the fair, buy candy.
Let's look to the hushed stars.)

[Gender. Sad.
Fair. No.
Stars. Maybe.]

Gender, fair, stars/stars, fair, gender.

Know. No.

The End

Savana Mazumder

<u>Untitled</u>

She threw the shotglass against the mirror
Not knowing we'd still be hearing it.
That fifty years would pass
And so much of gay and queer life would change
Some things astonishing and others stagnant.
In some places no one cares anymore
Others you can marry over a weekend
But lose your job on a Monday.
In some countries you might not be executed for it
(anymore)

For my part I'd known from childhood I was strange
But it wasn't until I heard my parents
jeering at the famous lesbian on TV
That I knew how my strangeness had to be secret.
I can still hear them
saying she must have tricked that poor girl
the poor girl who was beautiful
but somehow "that way"

I never told anyone except for my friends
Who didn't care
The reveal to them was easy,
But participating is always hard.
"I'm bisexual" does roll off the tongue
Though doing "gay stuff" is harder.
I worry that my bisexuality excludes me
Means I am an ill-fitting piece
Means I will never find my people
I worry that no matter how many glasses I break
The fractured reflection in the mirror
Will never be enough
Queer enough
Bi enough

Pan enough
Even nB trans enough.

Then I remember Marsha didn't feel enough
Not safe enough
Not human enough
Not worth enough to always be who she was.
And all I tell myself
is to keep breaking those shotglasses
Until the mirror is gone.
The mirror of "you're not queer enough"
Shattered
Until I can only see myself.

Pat McCutcheon

<u>Shared Custody, 1985: First Evening</u>

The red, green and yellow hammock
dipped across the living room.
Hollow-eyed, not eating dinner,
you sat on it, dear Sara,
eight years old, feet groping for the floor.
You clutched a gray stuffed rabbit
under your chin, and all the pink-cheeked,
brown-skinned dolls in gingham dresses,
stuffed bears and kittens
brought from your dad's, were tucked in
snug around you.
You sucked your thumb.
Blonde curls rumpled, pale skin,
blue-violet rings beneath your staring eyes.

Your mom and I love each other deeply.
I wonder if you'll ever come to understand
the love of two women.
Clinging by our fingernails, we believed
this would be a better life for you,
for your five-year-old brother Carl,
my freckled ten-year old Josh.

Dearest Sara,
how I wish I'd crouched down
beside you, on the carpet,
wrapped my arms around you,
nestled you back amid your menagerie,
and rocked you in the hammock
until the purple shadows beneath your blue eyes
disappeared.

After Reading "Even Cowgirls Get the Blues" While Happily Married

                    I.
I turn the pages hungrily,
savoring Tom Robbins' juicy prose,
anticipating my good friend Ruth's visit
when she and I'll discuss the novel.
Then comes page 152—
Sissy and Jellybean touching belly buttons,
kissing, lips mashing together, tongues tangling,
fingers fondling secret folds, crevices,
nipples, mounds – for four pages!
My breath grows short,
I read on quickly,
my panties damp.
Nothing like this in my Fundamentalist background!
Now I really want to see Ruth,
but not just for talking.
I loved her sharp mind, integrity,
cropped brown hair, her wit—
but this is different.
I want to touch her. Everywhere.
She'll be blown away. I am astounded myself.
We are both married after all.
She is coming to see our new son.
Lovemaking with my husband feels good.
I love him, don't I?

                    II.
The night I talk with Ruth
under the stars on the deck, she says, "Oh, no!
We'll talk more later."
We walk the next day to the back of the property,
sit on a redwood stump.
With tears in her eyes, she whispers,
"I have always loved women."
Twenty years older than me,
she'd lived loathing her desires,
years hating herself, losing jobs, friends.

Finally she married, had two daughters,
determined to suppress her feelings.
Wiping tears from her cheeks, I
move closer on the stump,
hold her sweat-shirted shoulders.
"It's different now," I plead,
"things have changed."
I speak of a new bisexual friend I've made,
a powerful lesbian poet I met.
Even the DSM with its official position
on homosexuality has changed.
My tentative fingers stroke
that soft, irresistible hair,
her quavering jawline,
the space where the delicate bones
at the base of her throat
almost meet.
"For years I've loved you, Ruth.
My church-raised mind is
madly trying to catch up,
but making love with you just feels
like it would be, well, wonderful and right!"
Days later, she teaches me to make love.
When I touch her,
she quivers, moans.
When she touches me,
I tremble.
Breathing her scent on my hands,
I awaken.
Like turning the page of a menu
having known only creamy vanilla,
I discover hot fudge.

<u>Joy</u>

Rumors of a cross burned on a gay doctor's lawn
greeted us in our new town, new life together.

Balloons and top down on our yellow convertible
first day that marriages were legal.

Those decades ago we vowed
in mental illness and in health,
in overdrafts and, if ever, wealth.

We worried about the rent, and whether our kids
were teased, why no one would hire you to teach.
We shouldered the shadow of that smoldering cross.

But worries didn't keep us from delight—
our first grader's card, "Merry Christmas, Two Moms!"
You teaching preschoolers patience with playdough.
Me feeling the familiar freckled Braille of your skin.

Into the lawn of our very own home
you mowed the word "JOY!"
Now you create a garden like a watercolor.
Aroma rises from two cups of French roast
beside our rumpled bed.
We linger, laugh at grandkids' photos, kiss,
reminisce about shadows overcome.

<u>Blues For Suzanne</u>

Young daughter of the Great Depression,
foraging for coal with your wagon
along Midwestern train tracks,
eating pheasant from traps in the vacant lot.
At twenty-two you headed to California,
enlisted in the Navy,
later ran a surf shop, designed wetsuits,
wrote for Cal Tech's Jet Propulsion Lab,
found your pagan tribe, your sacred rituals.
Published Plain Brown Wrapper,
fighting discrimination against
Gays and Lesbians in thirteen states,
and you nurtured the dying in an AIDS ward.
Met the woman who completed you,
a Wiccan ceremony celebrated your love
before you were allowed to marry.
Twenty-eight years cherished together,
six of them sharing your beloved
Charlynn's cancer journey.

After your inconsolable loss,
tall twentieth century Boadicea
mourning in your mobile home park,
I shared with you a bond-- we gathered monthly
with other crones around each other's tables.
Walking, you'd prop your large frame
with hands on two classy canes.
Your cropped brown hair above broad shoulders
loomed over us.
But your grief loomed even larger, loneliness
fathomless as the oceans you'd loved to sail.
Years of evenings without calls
you tried to fill with TV, DVD's and Facebook.
Even your beloved black lab Yma gone,
no one left to snuggle on the empty couch.
Mourning consumed you.
Then a stroke, a fall, a coma.

Days passed, silent but for Threshold Singers.
Friends surrounded your tilted bed.
Cheryl's palm patted your blanketed chest,
Jeff bent toward you, sang softly "Lean On Me,"
Ann rubbed vanilla-scented lotion
on your fisted hands, broad forehead
beneath graying hair.
Finally, as Bonnie played your favorite goddess chants,
Jennifer Berezan sang "She Carries Me to the Other Side."
You let yourself be carried.
You are free.

Now we sort through leftover
treasures of your story
in your crammed hoarder's nest.
The great love of your life shines through
in photos, wills, letters.
A Lesbian before Stonewall,
forging past burning crosses,
you gave us courage
pioneer, mentor, guide
for so many, for my wife and me.
May the circle be unbroken, Suzanne.
Blessed be.

Unsanctioned Epithalamium

for Cheryl

If we could marry,
I would write an epithalamium in praise
of twenty years, three children raised.
But our countrymen forbid us wedlock,
refuse to authorize the love of women.
So this is just a love poem,
strewn with breathless words,
first-days-of-frenzied-passion words,
panted in bold italicized delicious shivers,
phrases fierce as "I trust you."

Even after all these years,
this poem could never tell
how it feels to be utterly known--
beyond persona, make-up,
naked beneath my best impression--
still accepted without conditions.
Loved even,
in mental illness and in health,
in overdrafts and wealth,
through harried hugs and sideswiped kisses.

We chase our trials and errors,
ecstasies and terrors, try for balance, lose it,
mired in molasses, try to remember
what comes next or even where we put the list.
Decades ago, we swore each other all the love we had
before we knew how deeply we could love
anyone, could love ourselves. We made ends meet
with boxes of wine and frozen tubes of ground turkey,
around cheerleader practice and homework resistance
we wrote letters rustling with our passion.
Now we both truly know
what "I'll be there for you" means,
for better or for worse,

know what it promises,
only need a glance to say it.
If this were a paean to married love, one might look for
explicit scenes, straining with desire,
allusions to your blue eyes,
which, in certain light, turn thalo green
but, in any light, see straight through me.

This, however, is a discreet and decorous poem.
I'll mention just your hands. How they move me, my unwedded love.
Long-fingered, far-reaching, gardener's hands
that brush a hyacinth's tiny bulb with tenderness.
Your subtle fingers spread the supple soil, stroke a trough;
urgent, gentle touch pressing into moist, warm hunger;
the shaft grows deeper to enclose the alchemy. Heaven and earth
move.
The bulb wakes in darkness, into what she never knew was in her.
The air swells with ineffable fragrance, sweet, profound,
unauthorized, unsanctioned. We need no other license.

* * *

Sanctioned now, it's thirty-three years I praise!
Married at last, though still threatened,
the ecstasies and terrors fierce as ever.
We celebrate with wine from a bottle now,
delight in our children's children.

Stephen Mead

<u>Surpassing The Verdict</u>

How far these clouds go!
What's the best way to reach there?
Some laws fall like gravity.
They weight against trust.

Plant feet firmly, stand
rooted. Wide-eyed is
the opening of a heart.
Censorship stares down.
To oppress is to plug.

Yet, 'til death do us…

Offshoots spring forerunners
and to wed is to weave.

Such threads catch senses,
escape catchwords, reach beyond.

Perceive the subdued?

It's a transplanted pulse.
Plight blooms here
in blighting verdicts.

Through bars
the sky is seized.

That banner surpasses chloroform
smothering trumpets and tongues.

(For all international comrades living where it is illegal to be LGBT)

Lynn McGee

<u>A Texan Can't Live in New York City</u>

Tommy answered the door resplendent in a sundress, infant
sleeping in his arms. The baby's mother was setting out

plates, leaning across the dining room table, long hair
sweeping the glossy surface. Her photo, a black-and-white

head shot, joined the line of friends framed down his hallway;
theater people, like him, and some who stepped into shadow,

when he got sick. Tommy forgave everyone but himself.
He wrote in his journal about the night the virus claimed

his fate, the stranger who tenderly infected him. Like a woman
who feels the spark of conception in her body, he felt the cackle

of death in his veins. Tall, Texan, blond, he and his brother
picked me up at my parents' house in Dallas, and stood

in the living room, their cowboy boots leaving footprints
on the plush carpet. They were roommates, and we teased them

the way Texans tease other Texans, asking who got the big
bedroom—the oldest, of course. Tommy and I met

in Hollywood, acting class. I was Anne Frank and he was
Peter, kind beyond his years. He moved to New York before

I did and sent a postcard, sky scrapers leering down at a sexy
cowgirl — short skirt, suede fringe swinging as she flees in terror,

shag haircut framing Tommy's cutout face. *A Texan can't live
in New York City*, he captioned the image, and I fastened it

under plastic in the AIDS Quilt panel I made for him with my
nephew. We drew a yellow rose and the boy, eight years old

in a crew cut and begging to stay another week with me, as each
week passed, said it needed thorns. *Everyone has thorns*, he said.

Injury at the Beach

She resisted the end of summer,
put on a blue suit when beaches were closed
and willed her body to ride the whip between wave
and sky, entrusted her trajectory to waterfalls
of surf that shattered on shore—and that

was the beginning, and that was the end, her body
propelled with industrious torque and planted
at an angle no body would choose, her big
right shoulder breaking impact, bald head of bone
shrouded in blood as she made the long crawl ashore,

damaged land dweller intent on repair, and positioned
under harsh lights, limp arm taped to white walls
during x-rays, surgeons planting steel hooks. *First
you smell fat burning. Then they cut through muscle
and you smell steak. Then they cut through bone
and it smells like the dentist drilling.*

She tells me this in bed, after I bring coffee—
how she relearned to raise a mug and hold
a steering wheel, the shoulder her mother berated
for splaying the seams on girls' clothes, now
stitched tight as a football, red track glazed
and tender beneath my touch.

A Butch Woman Realizes Her Femme Girl Doesn't Get It

Because I keep my grip when she loses hers

Because I have a wider stance

Because I switch out our bicycle seats, adjust the gears
and pump the tires in the time it takes her to get dressed

Because the waiter calls me 'Sir'

Because a woman in the restroom calls security,
when I exit the stall

Because it's not the first time, this has happened

Because transmen think I'm one of them—

My lover doesn't bring me flowers.

She doesn't recognize my palette, the careful assembly
of fabric and hues that is part of my morning.

She doesn't see how small I am, beneath my silhouette,
and how large my love makes her.

When I'm gone, she'll miss something that wasn't there.

<u>A Transman Visits His Old School</u>

I visited my old neighborhood and school,
red brick and clanging gate. It was Open House
and the concrete walls flapped with paper
hands, hearts and portraits of the self.
I remember art class, the smell of finger paints
and wielding the fat brush, chunky cylinders
of chalk. Eyes were easy—almonds, circles;
brows a pair of orange rinds, hair a scribbled
nest. Kids still title their self-portraits, *I am
a girl,* or *I am a boy,* each child choosing a side,
a path thick with onlookers cheering in love
and menace. I drew what was expected of me.
I remember picture books, the reading rug,
our teacher turning pages and me cross-legged
at her feet, putting myself in the illustrations
but keeping it a secret—the husband, the father
I envisioned becoming, even as I printed
above my drawing: *I am a girl.*

<u>We Fight</u>

In fourth grade, girls had to wear a skirt
or dress, so I wore a skirt
over my pants. My mom didn't notice—
she was a drug addict, sick in bed
all day while I settled fights
in the schoolyard, my little sister
Carrie on the sidelines crying
and the other kids yelling, *Punch him
in the face, Punch him in the stomach.*
Sometimes we met on the baseball field.
The diamond tilted downhill, dirt
and weeds and crumbling, white lines.
I was the only girl who could fist fight
instead of jumping in windmill-style,
and I felt conflicted about a fight I had
agreed to, with Mary Flynn. I kind of
had a crush on her and besides, I was
afraid her older sister would intervene,
but she didn't and I won, which means
the loser calls out, *I surrender*
and the loser's friends walk home
solemnly while the winner enjoys
neighborhood fame for a week
or so. That felt good. Also I was
super proud of my baseball skills.
I could hit and throw really hard.
Our other activity was sleepovers
at Debbie Leon's house; older sister
Susan, younger sister Nel. I was totally
in love with her, too. We would go in
her parent's room, get the *Playboy*s
out from under the bed and make out
while the other girls poured crème
de menthe over ice cream and danced
in the kitchen. My father was in Vietnam,
which you could watch on TV at dinner
and wonder if that was him,

in the black-and-white explosions.
My stepfather managed the motel
next door. He would pin me to the wall
of the swimming pool and my mom
was back in the hospital when he got
in bed with me the first time,
touching me with one hand and holding
a cigarette with the other. I had this
beat-up desk I pushed in front
of the door, after that. I grabbed him
by the hair, once, from the backseat
and slammed his head against
the driver's side window—*bam,*
bam,bam. He pulled over and made
my mom drive, his hand on the lighter
shaking. He would leave for a couple
days—we never knew where, but you
would see him peeking
in the living room windows. I was
always on the lookout for him
and meanwhile kept tabs on the bullies
at school. Chuckie Carson was stocky
and strong, and mean to my younger
sister, an easy target—super scrawny,
legally blind, thick fucking glasses.
After school, I'd make her take them
off and catch a softball with me.
If she cried, I'd yell, *Toughen up.*

Glenn McMurray

<u>The Ward</u>

the doors were locked and guarded
he locked them and kept watch
cameras dotted along the corridors
ensuring there's no botched
attempt at cheating the rules
taking him for a fool
made to look stupid
by a queer little kid
the jailor's ridicule

one day the jailor was enlightened
found out after all this time
he's been keeping under lock and key
a secret so sublime
it's a wonder that only now
that part of him is allowed
to step out the door
unclothed, cocksure
without even a towel

now every day of every week
is strip off, suck-off Sunday
doors unlocked, cameras off
the jailor made to pay
for hiding queer boy inside
forbidding him to confide
in anyone alive
thirty-five fucking
years of swallowed pride

and the jailor's punishment?
the torment – of finding out exactly
how toothsome boys can be
exposed to the gnarly

nature of bathhouse sex
nameless men, no regrets
stroke and shove
mouthing love
to gain the boy's respect

<u>Dandy</u>

in my twenties
he appeared in my dreams
then in my groin
how i loved his honesty
bold and brave
unafraid
we'd skip hand in hand
oh, the fun we had

then directly after it seems
i'd don a mask
mannequin impaled on a stand
rebuff him
pretend
that i didn't understand
how we could have been so bad

in my thirties
he appeared in the white space
then in my words
like my ink was his blood
fragile and fey
hiding
looking for a way to say
remember me?

when creativity took place
and my writing
had a hint of something
that could
unlock
those things so far away
he held a key

in my forties
he appears beside me
like an aura

ready to be embodied
warm and tactile
human
arisen through my keyboard
confident, quaint and free

but our heart might break in three
if it ends
and he'll weep ink and blood
into white
pulp
screwed up, aptly ignored
the way i used to be

in my fifties
he'll appear through art
bristles tickling canvas
his blood running through
my hand and
brush
with a colourful demeanour
dancing gayly in a frame

i'll have captured him
after his flight of fancy
placed him in a cage
where he sings
bird-like
pecking his image in the mirror
happily without shame

David Messineo

<u>*Friendship and Freedom*</u>, Christmas Eve 1924, Chicago, Illinois

Remembering the true start of the American gay rights movement, and honoring its forthcoming 100th anniversary in 2024

Illinois issues us a charter, a starter to barter
into paid memberships. I'll start with a newsletter
called *Friendship and Freedom* this Christmas Eve, no better
way to spread word. Write/publish two issues, no plan to be martyr,
just dedicate my energy to a principle of fairness - full, true equality
belongs to women who love women, men who love men, "queers."
But America would bootstamp my cause for a full 25 years,
with FBI, CIA, and the words THREAT TO NATIONAL SECURITY.

<u>Bayard Rustin Organizes the 1963 March on Washington</u>

"I have a dream!" he thundered to thousands,
but even The Great Reverend was no saint.

Seeing "them" arrive on hundreds of buses to
organized barricades, ample bathrooms,
white America predicted all kinds of horror,
as the unenlightened typically do. What they *saw*
were neatly dressed people, intent listening,
few if any problems: a masterpiece of theater
staged for television and a world audience.
Dazzled by Doctor King, few wondered
how it all happened. How, the hundreds of
bathrooms? How, the neat box lunches?

Bayard Rustin. His name was Bayard Rustin.
Tall, thin, African-American, intellectual,
spectacled "point man" for Doctor King,
Bayard brought together all the details:
leading, partnering, successfully coordinating
a flawless "invasion" the scale of Normandy
onto the National Mall, the Lincoln Memorial.

Essayist, author, brilliant speaker,
ask most Americans: "Never heard of him."
But he made history. "Never heard of him."
"Never heard of him" because of his selfless act.

Determined to derail Doctor King's movement,
when he couldn't nail COMMUNISM
to Martin Luther King's cross,
J. Edgar Hoover tried a different sign:
a label of HOMOSEXUAL nailed
to Martin Luther King's strategist.

Fearing that accurate tar brush, fearing it could
undermine the Civil Rights movement
just as that Freedom Train was gaining traction,
Bayard Rustin offered his resignation, after years
of service, guidance, loyalty, to Doctor King.
Doctor King accepted Rustin's resignation.

Martin Luther King asked us to imagine the day
when justice would roll upon us like a mighty stream.
Now that that tide at long last has begun to turn,
perhaps it's time to acknowledge, remember, *thank*
the homosexual who helped channel all that water.

<u>The Price That Finally Killed Bob Barker</u>

"You are the first four contestants on
'The Price Is Right.' And now, here is
the star of 'The Price Is Right,' Bob Barker!"
An eruption of applause, a bow.

"These four people are in line
to win some fabulous prizes today
on 'The Price Is Right'!
Let's see the first item up for bid!"

The giant double doors open onto
Rachel Reynolds, alone on stage.
Confused, Bob asks, "Rachel,
where is the first item up for *bid*?"

Rachel smiles, gracefully arcs her arm.
"Well, the first item up for bid
is so large, Bob, it doesn't *fit*
on our stage!"

"So large it doesn't fit on our stage?
That hasn't happened in 35 years!
Audience, are you excited?
I'm excited! *Whatever* can it *be*?"

Rachel smiles, arcs her arm again,
her sequined dress glimmering in
the studio lights. "Let's have the camera
show them the prize!"

The camera cuts to people. Thousands
of people, all wearing uniforms. Soldiers.
Sailors. Pilots. Nurses. Coast Guard.
Army. Marines. Shined shoes. Spiffy.

"Who are all these people?" Bob asks.
"I'm Margarethe Cammermeyer,"
one replies. "The 10,000 of us here
outside Bob Barker Studio are up for bid."

"We don't sell people on this show,"
Bob replies. "We sell refrigerators,
boats, a *new car*! But I'll play along: how
do I explain your price to our contestants?"

"Well, Bob, it's quite simple. The 10,000 of us were
thrown out of the U.S Armed Forces for
being gay or lesbian. The 10,000 of us here
are the price of American prejudice."

Bob doesn't know *what* to say, so he
does what he does best. He smiles, continues,
"The price of American prejudice.
Contestant #1, what is your bid?"

After taking four bids, rangingfrom
$99,999 to $1 (a 'Price Is Right' strategy),
Bob turns to Margarethe, who replies,
"Sorry, Bob. None are even close."

Bob's turn: "Well, this electronic panel
where we display prices only can go
up to five digits. What do you suggest?"
"Have the number represent millions, and bid again."

"Millions?" Bob looks incredulous.
"*Millions??*" Ten thousand people
look at each other and nod. Bob
looks at them as Margarethe says, "Millions."

"Do you mean to tell me that
the cost to American taxpayers to
throw all you fine people out of service
exceeds *one million dollars*?"

She nods. He takes four bids,
ranging from 2 to 285.
"All right, let's have it - what is
the price of American prejudice?"

"From 1994 to 2006, the cost to
find replacements, retrain personnel,
hold court cases, pay attorneys, all add up
to a grand total of one - billion - dollars."

"One billion dollars?" Bob stammers,
his suntan shading red. *One billion??!*"
And the audience screams as Bob ends
35 years of service, crashing to the floor.

<u>17 in '79</u>

In memory of Sylvester James (d. December 16, 1988)

In a baby blue room carpeted blue-black tweed,
my first "stereo of my own" moment - a CLICK. The
J.C. Penney stereo/turntable pumps warm green light,
comforting glow against darkness, offering a strange sound
I couldn't describe, almost like wind, then a sudden
wall of rhythm and clacking, a clarion call to something new
yet primal, compelling and magical. The year - 1977.
The song - "I Feel Love" by Donna Summer.

1979. I suspect my mother is downstairs in the kitchen,
sifting through "P" in the *Yellow Pages* for "Psychologists."
She will hush her voice, express sincere concern
that I have listened to the same song seventeen times
in a row. Why her teenage Italian-American son
is now so enthralled by a black gospel/disco group is
beyond both of us at the moment, battle ablaze between
its *dance the beat in the disco heat* and her *"TURN THAT DOWN!"*

Vicki Sue Robinson turned the beat around, while the starched-shirt
public wanted it all turned off. DISCO SUCKS T-shirts
capitalized their way into my high school, and a disco album
burning at a Chicago ballpark led to mayhem and blood. Donna
Summer would go rock, then born again, yet sustain her career
into six decades. My father was wrong, as usual:
Donna would last longer than Elvis (Elvis, 1953-1977,
24 recording years. Donna, 1968-2011, 42 recording years.),

But in '79 at 17, it was Sylvester and Two Tons O'Fun,
Martha Wash and Izora Rhodes, forging their unmatched gospel/disco
three-part-harmony wall of vocal power and exuberant sound, chanting
dance the beat in the disco heat, come on,
and we did, hundreds of us on the dance floors
across America, around the world, hypnotized by
Patrick Cowley on synthesizer, Tip Wirrick on guitar, disco's
Dynamic Duo, supporting disco's one true male star, Sylvester James,

falsetto from heaven with a Liberace-lavish lifestyle. Cowley
died first, November '82, age 32, in the first wave. Sylvester,
in '88. Much of his audience in between. While Rock Hudson
denied to death, Sylvester asked to be photographed in *People*:
"I don't want my friends to get this. Make sure they see it."
There'd be worse musician/role models, but that wasn't why I listened.
In their music, *I* was in the back seat of a Volkswagen between two
big black women, all four of us heading to a Marin County audition.

In their joy, in their music, I was *not* in my high school's cinder block
prison. I was anywhere, anywhere, anywhere but there.

<u>Imprinting</u>

From fingerprints, we watch her face unfold
to wrinkles, gestures, eyes that penetrate,
that put me in a contemplative state.
Your fingers at your side - will I be bold
enough to hold your hand in here? So old
this scene, this melodrama played from date
to date - a Chuck Close retrospective, great
dramatic backdrop this time, I am told -

or, rather, overhear, a little to
my right - a man and woman, holding hands,
who seem the type to whisper, point, then preen.
My eyes take in *your* eyes - it's all I do.
Then we absorb her eyes. *She* understands
the many ways art permeates a scene.

Michael Montlack

<u>*Female Trouble*: Dawn Davenport (Divine)</u>

You didn't just open my suburban window—
you smashed it with one clumsy Kung Fu kick,
in the Cha Cha heels your parents refused to buy
for Christmas. At 13 how I wanted to dash
down that vanilla street with you in nothing
but a baby doll nightie and fuzzy blue slippers—
my backside the last damn thing those smalltown drones
would see of me—a blur of bouffant, boobs
and beergut wrapped in chiffon, certain one day
they'd bow before me, a hush stuck in their throats
like the bones of a rotten fish while I'd scowl as if
I'd just eaten dog shit, repeating a sing-song *fuck you*
so discordant, only the strayest cats would dare
follow me home.

Questions My Father Asked Watching *This Old House*

That afternoon I was beside him on my mother's half of their bed.

Our English Setter licking his gnarly unsocked feet.
While host Bob Vila sang the praise of plaster over stucco.
My father shaking his head on the pillow, Camel wedged in lips:
"Plaster? This knucklehead doesn't know what he's talkin' about."

I never asked why he watched so religiously if he doubted
Bob's every move. Never agreed or disagreed, knowing
nothing about home repair myself. Just used the show's half-hour
as I had since junior high: a way to be near.

"So let me ask you something," he started.

The plaster was being mixed. The dog continued to lick.

Out just weeks, this was what I'd been waiting for: The inevitable
"So do you … do drag?" Or … "You one of those, um, leather guys?"

My father, a mechanic in his 60's, hadn't known openly gay people.

But no.

He said: "Why are gay people smarter than straight people?"

I hesitated. Swallowed the impulse to vent about all the *himbos*
I'd met my few months going to bars. "We aren't," I said.
Realizing his reasoning: Me, the family's first degree.
"It's just easier to come out in educated circles."

The walls nearly primed. The dog paused to lick his own foot.

"So then … why are you guys always more creative?"
I wasn't prepared. Having only rehearsed vows to use condoms.
And settle down one day.

"Well, I guess being silenced," I said, "we use the arts to express?"

Bob had spatula in hand. Making circular patterns.
Pleased with himself.

"I mean, there are gay migrant workers," I added. "But who can they tell?"

He rolled his head on the pillow to look my way. Camel burned out.
                              "Well, how come you're not angry?"

And then: I was back at his station, all those summers pumping gas.
Collecting tips just for being Howie's son. Nine, ten, eleven years old.
Had they been cosmic compensation? For ignoring his crew in the shop:
This fan belt's a real cocksucker! When's that faggot coming for his Pinto?

I couldn't answer. Did this mean I wasn't angry? Surely
I'd met guys with chips on their shoulders. Guys who drank their chips away.
Where was my chip? Still in the closet? In my writing? The need to write?

Bob was in different clothes now. On a return visit. The walls fully dried.

"No," I said finally. "I guess I'm not angry."

But what could I be angry about? There, so comfortable in that bed.
With my father and his dog. Learning how to build a more beautiful home.

Homosexuality

So long at the bottom of the well—
occasional shafts of sunlight
disturbing the darknesss—my eyes
calibrated to decipher shadows
for other nocturnal creatures.

Always there were none.

When the rope finally lowered,
I was so delirious with fever
I nearly looped my neck with it,
instead of my waist, expecting
to be booby-trapped at the top.

It's okay. I'll get you outta there!
The voice familiar—my own?
Maybe. I'd never really heard
what I sounded like. Unless this
was the trap? Wait! Too late—

he was pulling me through
the well's mouth. Gathering me
into his arms. *Breathe. Breathe.*
Everything seemed jeweled
with a glare. Even his badge.

Engraved with my name?

Preoccupied by the charge
I inherited, I almost forgot
my note scratched nightly
into the well's stone walls:
By the time you read this ...

Scars in my fingerprints.

<u>¿Comprende?</u>

Tamika said I could come
to her family barbeque
as long as I didn't tell
the kids at school.
I figured she meant the pig
spinning on the spit
like those golden bangles
on the loose hairy wrists
of her Tios Fernando and Roberto
who pulled Tamika's mother
onto the patio 'dance floor'
of her crowded backyard
whenever Tito Puente
blared from the transistor,
the two men, arms flailing,
sandwiching her, passing
her back and forth, the way
Tamika and I shared colas.

Where are your Tias? I asked.
Don't they have wives?

She looked down
at my empty paper plate.
Mas arroz con pollo?

<u>Daddy: A Delicate Diatribe</u>

Yeah, crawl a little closer,
and you just might detect
a whiff of lavender oil
in my whip's handle,
or, maybe if you're lucky,
some stubborn glitter
to lick from my boot sole.

Don't make me tell you
again: *DUNGEON RULES*
on the cinderblock walls:
a rainbow of pastel chalks,
the barback's penmanship
elegant as Grandmama's.

And don't be afraid—
let all your power slide
like a bra strap, so demure,
over that furry shoulder.
Just don't make me tell you
again. Whimper and I'll
hear only manliness. Cling
like a barnacle to my calf—
I'll gauge your strength.

Press the right button, pig,
and I might weep with you.
Tugging you closer. Closer.
So you can inhale the musk
of my hairy nipple, allowing
me to serve while you nurse.

Louise Moore

<u>Problems With Parts</u>

My mechanic tells me
it is the bent pulley
on the alternator
that caused
my serpentine belt
to break.
The part can be replaced.

Body parts aren't that easy.
To get bad cells to die
and not keep replicating like
rabbits
We poison
cut or radiate.

Dorothy don't
tap your ruby slippers
3 times yet.

We have hearts
aren't straw
and don't want you to
fly away in the morning.

<u>For Betty Bacall</u>

It is the era
of Maltese Falcon

All the gay girls
want to meet Betty Becall.

All the gay boys want to
live in the Colony with
up and comings
Rock Hudson Tony Perkins.

But really
the gay boys
would love to suck off
Bogart.
When they are old men
they'll claim they did.

Our managers make sure we
act straight.

We could still go out
to the Springs for the weekend
to play
The reporters kept their mouths shut
and Preston wrote in jokes
into his scripts.

In my dream
I am one of the gang.
Straight teeth
tan
blond and high heeled.

In my dreams
I am refined
there are no bottles clinking

by the bed
Only women
in it
With smoky voices
like Betty Becall.

Tal Moskowitz

<u>Be You</u>

I walked to school
with all my stuff
I wasn't in a big rush
I went inside
And took a seat
I looked in my bag
For something to eat
Everybody asked "what's on your nails?"
I said "There's not much details"
"I painted my nails" is what I said
Everybody stared up at my head
Then two of my friends came up and said
"Why are you so astonished?"
"He is allowed to wear nail polish!"

Emmet Munroe

<u>Peeking Out</u>

It's 20-flipping-19
And here I am, still chilling in the closet.
It's cozy in here…
if not a little cramped.
Here I admire the things I put on:
Carefully planned and pressed outfits,
And my stealthily stashed dildo collection
Ahem…
It's 20-flipping-19
I know at least 3 happily married gay couples,
And gay coaches,
And a gay Sunday School Teacher,
And my gay sister.
But not me. Not just yet.
It's 20-flipping-19
It's never been better to be gay
It's never been LESS taboo
Or more posh, or fleek, or…fabulous!!
Ahem…
It's 20-flipping-19
Soon I'll be 20-flipping-9 years old...
So why is this closet door jammed?

<u>Gayly Ever After</u>

They lived gayly ever after.
Words that I've only whispered to myself in my pillow
When I'm dreaming of those chivalrous straight princes
Who will never be mine.
The childish ideal of Cinderella…
Reality sets in.
Alone watching gay porn, asking myself
Is this Happily Ever After for me?
They lived gayly ever after
And I dream of those childhood ideals…
Tarzan held Jane so close, her safety more important than his own
Telling myself this IS
That same magical love
While a stranger pins me down,
Climaxes,
And leaves without a single kiss.

<u>I Heard A Student Call Someone "Faggot"</u>

I heard a student call someone "faggot"
As a new teacher, I froze awkwardly
"You're the adult now." I told myself "You're the boss."
"Teach them what your peers never did"
"If nothing else, just shout 'HEY!'"
"Like you wish your teachers did for you"
"When you hated yourself back in middle school."
"And hid during High School"
"When you still today hold that fear."
"Now it's time to step up."
Before I responded I heard something.
Not a second after that first remark,
Even louder, deeper in sound, from his classmate
"Seriously dude. No one says that."
"Right." Said another, "Not cool."
It was done.
The fear, the shame, the ignorance, the hate
The cycle died…
Ended!
By students.

<u>Embracing</u>

I hugged another man in public,
And felt safe in his caressing arms.
Protected in his tight squeeze
The knight of my dreams

Now I can savor every second
Without the fear
That our arms twisting together publicly
Will create crosshairs on our backs

I can smell the musk of his cologne
And ignore the mummers of the busy street around us
Embracing this moment
Safely nestled in his arms
Just another passionate couple
Just another PDA

<u>We Are Standing on the Shoulders of Queens</u>

We are standing on the shoulders of Queens!
Who flaunted what so many feared
Who stomped out of the secrecy of clubs
And down the main streets in their sharpest stilettos
Each mighty step sounding
like the crushing of close-minded bones beneath their heals

We are standing on the shoulders of Bears
Who bravely fought for what was right
Fought for their survival
For all of us to exist

We are still standing
Lifted up by real, brave, powerful men and women
Strong enough to take a stand not for themselves
Not for their close ones
But for all of us
So that 50 years later
People like me can be proud to step up to this mantel
And be fierce
And be free
And be me

Joseph Munisteri

<u>Butterfly</u>

I saw something beautiful,
flapping its wings.
At first, it was only a glimpse.
Swooping past me,
just out of sight.
But it was just enough,
to get my attention.
When I finally saw it,
it spread its wings.
Colors galore, like a rainbow on each wing.
As I investigated further,
it turned out to be,
A butterfly staring back at me.
I see its scared,
as beautiful as it may be.
As I get closer,
I stare back into its eyes,
as I am caught by surprise.
Through them, I am shocked,
by what I see,
I see me.

~ Previously published in *Butterflies in Space*

<u>Queer Imaginings</u>

Two minds gather,
Filled with the absurd,
Ironic and sometimes,
Straight up bluntness,
They form a think tank,
Forming a cannon of ideas,
Before they know it,
Others gather,
Not fully understood,
They prepare to fire,
using a cannonball filled with their queer imaginings,
into a crowd that hadn't understood them,
Hoping the explosion it creates,
Would help them understand,
The insights from thoughts and ideas of the
"Not Normal"

~ Previously published in *Butterflies in Space*

Erica Nicole

<u>Growing Up Queer</u>

Growing up queer is
learning how to love yourself
without example.

<u>Dyke</u>

"Dyke."
The word spat onto me
with the kind of disgust only a mother could muster.
I was fourteen,
felt more at home in a button down than any dress I had ever been
squeezed into.

This time,
the dress was green.
It was hers, back when she was her mother's perfect daughter-
Something I could never be.
I think she was hoping the dress had magic powers,
could make me
more straight hair and straight-laced
and straight.
Make me feel
more girl,
less imposter.
More seen, not heard; more delicate and satin,
less rough around the edges.

I think she thought that if I acted like a girl
I wouldn't want to kiss them.
Maybe,
I would stop feeling so out of place in this costume of a body I was
supposed to fit in.

I think I wore a skirt that day;
it was the only agreement that could be made.
It seemed easier to breath in
-the closest thing to a two-piece suit she'd ever let me wear.
It felt like compromise:
A mother and daughter celebrating together,
picture perfect polaroid of a lie frozen in time.
My mom tells me about lies and omitting the truth;
tells me there's a difference,
that no one needed to know

I felt different.

She called it a phase.

Fast Forward.

I lay in bed with a man I might love,
dress and heels thrown on the floor,
makeup still done...
I play this role so well, I forget when it started to feel like truth;
like I was no longer playing dress-up in my mother's life.
I know she'd be proud of me
if i told her.
But twenty-five year old me feels guilty for falling for a man when
fourteen year old me had to take a beating for loving a girl and twenty-
seven year old me will probably have to explain why I can't
"just pick a side".

I look at that green dress still hanging in my closet a decade later,
and I start to think my mother was right.
I almost forget about the nights I cried myself to sleep
or the morning I threw up in the car because I knew I'd have to tell the
girl I loved it was over.
But then I remember a friend telling me that if you say a lie out loud
enough times, it becomes true.
And how many times did she make me say
        I'm straight.
        The girl meant nothing to me.
        Kissing her was a gross mistake.
        I am a good Catholic girl, a good Italian daughter.

If you ask my mother now,
she will tell you that none of this happened.
Not the silent car rides
or the forced penance
or the yelling
or the beating
She will tell you that she loves me *unconditionally.*

She will not tell you she was going to kick me out of her house for
wearing my pride to the family barbeque
or that she called me a cold-hearted bitch when I didn't apologize for
it.

The one thing
we will both tell you
is that my mother
didn't raise
no
dyke.

<u>Dyke (Part II) or What I Think My Mother Meant</u>

"Dyke".
And I mean:
Disgusting
Disaster
Dishonor
Defective

I mean,
I look at my daughter
and don't understand how she could be so selfish

I thought I drowned this out of her months ago
Convinced myself this horror would dissipate into nothing more than a
nightmare
But here she is
wearing my disappointment like a new button down
She seems so determined to be my undoing

Doesn't she know what people will say about me?
How inadequate I will look?
I can't even raise my daughter right?
After everything I've sacrificed for her,
how hard would it be to surrender me this?

To live without love is this family's destiny.
It is our women's birthright.
We do what is dignified
not what is desired

I tell her she is disgraceful
Her actions are worthy of disownment
and I mean it
Even if I never dare say it outside of this home
I mean it

I call my daughter a dyke
hoping she will know just how much I despise what she has become

<u>An Open Letter to Randy Weber</u>

At a religious rights activist event in Washington DC, Texas state representative Randy Weber tearfully altered the Lord's prayer to beg forgiveness for the sin of marriage equality.
Randy Weber says that marriage is between man and woman.
Feels that there should be no protection for anyone that identifies differently.

In response to Mr. Weber's false prayers

I know what it's like to stand in the fire
to love a woman with such conviction, some would like to see us set ablaze
When I moved from New York to Texas
there were *certain* parts of the country my girlfriend and I were scared to get out of the car in
The only thing worse than being a gay couple in a homophobic state
is that state believing in open carry.
       We got out of the car anyway
       She held my hand anyway
       Heathens need bathroom breaks too, don't we?

Or are we less than human?
Does that make it easier to hate me?
Without even knowing my name
would you convict me?

Use scripture for kindling at the witch burning
Hold the cross like a bludgeon
Pray I don't get too much of this sinner's blood on your shoes

You said "we must create a culture of life so that every life is cherished and protected".
In the same breath you called on us to help preserve traditional marriage
Told us it was the only way to keep American families strong
My Aunt Mary & Uncle Frank were married for almost 70 years before he died.

They had 2 children.
He had a government job.
Even in their 80s he would still smile and call her his girl.
My Aunt Mary says that everyone finds happiness differently. That true love is a gift. She tells me not to settle for anything less than what she had.
And I know what she means is someone who loves me through everything.
And body parts have nothing to do with that.

I think you're scared Mr. Weber.
Scared of the kind of love that has never needed a certificate or a ring to stay strong.
The kind of love that can't be shocked out of us.
Isn't it surprising to you that we still haven't given up yet?

Isn't that what a strong American family should look like?
Never giving up on each other no matter what obstacles are thrown our way.

You tell us that your god hates us;
that we will burn in hell;
that we must repent if we want a chance at heaven.

If I was a praying woman, Mr. Weber

I still would not ask for your understanding
or for your god's forgiveness.
I will not apologize for believing in love
I sleep just fine at night, no matter who is sleeping next to me
I do not fear the dark because I am surrounded by light.

I can respect your life, even if I don't agree with it.
Funny how a sinner can follow God's word better than you can.
But then again, it was a sinful woman who witnessed the resurrection who loved with such conviction that no false prophet could ever bring her shame.

You make fallacy out of faith Mr. Weber.
And I'll be Damned before I ever believe in you.

<u>Chimera</u>

Chimera

(noun)

Definition: an illusion or fabrication of the mind

Definition: anything composed of very disparate parts or perceived as wildly imaginative, implausible or dazzling

Definition: a fire breathing she-monster in Greek mythology having a lion's head, a goat's body, and a serpent's tail

Queer:

(adjective)

Definition: differing in some odd way from what is usual or normal

Definition: something that is odd, different, strange or non-mainstream

Definition: originally pejorative for gay, now being reclaimed as a self-affirming umbrella term for any member of the LGBTQIA* community

Chimera

(Noun)

Queer

(Adjective)

Funny how both can be monster or creation

To be queer is to be a misunderstood myth
To be feared
Or dismissed

Made of parts the world will tell us don't match

In Greek mythology,
Seeing a chimera was an omen for disaster

Disaster

(noun)

Definition: an accident or trouble

My family carries my queerness tucked inside their cheeks
The words don't roll easily off their tongues
They are afraid to unleash catastrophe
On any unsuspecting victim that might behold me

Queer

(verb)

Definition: to spoil or ruin

Some days
I feel more science project than human
More monster
More mashing together of things that don't go
More queering everything I touch
But I am more than a fantasy
My existence is not lore

I will not be silenced

Silence

(verb)

Definition: to prohibit or prevent from speaking
Definition: to stop the noise of

Belleraphon's greatest feat was killing Chimera
He shot a leaded arrow into her throat
I will not choke on the weight of my words the way Chimera was
forced to swallow her own lava

Anyone can be made a monster if you do not understand them
But I will not be defined by the ways I hold myself together

Casey Oraa

<u>Still Here</u>

Rendered invisible
By time and by privilege
My needs do not change
While others get theirs.
Bitter, I'm not.
Affected, I am.
I work, I toil!
Marriage for some, jail for others
Bricks within which we're all contained.
Our struggle is shared,
But do you see it that way?

<u>So-so-so</u>

Police in parades
Police on parade
Draped in rainbows, shooting...
Water guns,
What a splendid sight!
To some.
But what's this? Exclusion?
No, it's Equity,
The less attractive cousin of Equality
Which challenges all your excess in order to
Just ask for the basics:
Respect, stability, dignity,
A place to safely lay one's head
That isn't a cell, a shelter or
A street corner.
Gays on parade, confetti in the gutters
A mere dressing that glazes over the reality
We're not all "equal"
We're not all "together"
Some of us still need
Your active solidarity.

<u>In Motion</u>

Sailing through the air
A reddish, solid mass
Now a mythical symbol
The brick that was thrown.
But can our successes and failures
Be attributed to just one person, one thing?
There are key moments for sure
But isn't it about the "us", the "we"?
When did we fall into the trappings of that we resist?
The brick never landed. It didn't.
As long as there are "us" and "we".

<u>It's In The Minutes</u>

Across the room you all stand
A chasm between us
A sea of mostly gay white men
All in a rage.
Salivating over the power
That you perceived you had and is now gone,
Your false cover for your false solidarity.
"Inclusion", you scream.
"Safety!", we scream.
A pause takes over after one of you spills your latte.
A few attempts, to traverse the waters between us,
But if someone doesn't care about your safety and security,
How can you really even have a dialogue?
The meeting is over, what did we achieve?
Another set of minutes, another false promise of hope.

Joshua Sassoon Orol

<u>Trans Girl at the National Gallery</u>

I never got to roll my eyes at Georgia O'Keefe
and her colorful vaginal blooms
because I was too busy improvising prayers—
May it be a simple truth that not everything
is unyielding, erect, and unwept as me.

I can't figure out why the boys in Hopper's *Ground Swell*
stare at the crests, the tilting iron channel buoy,
the hard blue line of horizon, why stare at anything
other than her wide, white back.
Straight men crave women in a way that's never
about finding one more black box full of dress up,
one quiet closet where lace goes unremarked.

<u>Shoshana's Tongue</u>

Trust me when I say
Josh has longed for tits and hips
and all night
for the oasis between my legs
but of all my parts
he's imagined most
                my tongue--

muscular changeling
        moshpit tongue

can scream like heels on the street
        can also sweet sing tongue

altar of unhewn stones
                dirt caked tongue

four cornered prayer
    wrap your family in it tongue

laugh too loud and get hurt for it tongue

Gramma worries it's too thin
        has it been eating enough
tongue?

        Lip licking tongue
    Wrestle with god tongue
    raise up the kids tongue
trope chanting tongue

pleasure center of the body
        let it go all soft and fat
    fluid tongue

Leave it on the lip
until it dries white
    you can watch dreams ripple
across the subvocal tongue

Name it once more
that body part you crave:
Wet, sassy, a girl's favorite color.

Emory Parker

<u>We Don't Hold Hands</u>

Every day
We put on a show
Our best poker face
An award-winning act

We try not to break
When they ask if we're
Sisters
Roommates
Friends

We don't hold hands in daylight
We don't sit close on subways
We don't picnic in the park

We can't

Not anymore

When rights are stripped away
Every hour of every day
Who's to say
We'll be okay
What's the price we'll have to pay

Make America Hate Again

But, we'll always have night

Safe
Out of the spotlight
In darkness
Under the stars

We play hide and seek
And stealthily sneak
Around dumpsters
Behind cars
Kids after curfew
Just trying to catch a break
Catch a breath

Breathe

But, sometimes, at night
Hellish creatures come out
Rats and vermin
Scour the street
For a nibble
For a bite
Of what they can't have

They taunt
And they tease
Putting hands and teeth
Where they're not welcome

Sniffing
Licking
Devouring
The meat
Until it's just scraps
Until they collapse

We don't hold hands in daylight
We don't go out at night
We stay out of trouble
Until wrong is right

Kenneth Pobo

<u>Child of an Older Man of Stonewall</u>

On June 28, 1969, I was 14.
My Illinois life
was Tommy James and the Shondells
who had just released "Crystal Blue
Persuasion." Tommy sang of peace
and good, brotherhood. I like peace

though not the kind that drops
into a Lazy Boy and shuts the light off.
That peace can make us die.
At Stonewall, we told the cops no,
we won't be invisible. Our colors
have always been bright no matter
who comes at us with billy clubs.

At 14 I didn't know I was gay,
didn't know what gay means.
I thought I was *different.*
The God of my church wanted me
to be a graham cracker, every one
in the box the same. The Stonewall

protesters fought several hundred
miles away. When I hold
my husband's hand I know that
Stonewall hasn't ended. We stand
before a poison tide of hate and
don't run away. The shore isn't safe.
We repeat the names of our dead,
walk beside our young.

<u>Faggot Poems</u>

Today's rejection says: "We don't
publish any faggot poetry." So
poetry has a sexual preference—

good to know. It's true
that two poems reflected on
a relationship. The word penis
didn't come up or should I say rise?
The other three poems were
1) about a bluebird,
2) about mom hanging laundry, and
3) a homeless Philly man asking for a buck.

Were those faggot poems too? Maybe
the editor also writes poems, lines coming
from Hooters. My gay songs go out,
the page a deepening lavender.

<u>Wilde Strawberries</u>

I find I'm in a Bergman film.
I'm not dreaming. I somehow
unstitched my life and

here I am, an old professor,
and though I've lived selfishly
near the end I confront that
and get a childhood scene
of my parents, only wait,
it's not my folks, it's Oscar Wilde
and Sappho saying witty things
in a countryside with lavender
flowers turning into rockets
that take us above Earth
but we can't live up there,
not yet, so we come down

to where a tres gay river
runs past a tres gay fern—
we're no longer unnatural,
we never were, all of the blooming
world walks, runs on the wild side—

my man pops out
from behind only the most fabulous
birch tree ever, takes my hand,
and the film ends

like a stone giving
birth to several still lakes.

Michael Allen Potter

<u>The Elusive Nomenclature of Two Unmarried Men on an American Train Before Equality</u>

I have been trying to describe America without the words 'wide' or 'open' or 'spaces,' have been trying to keep g*d from possessing my country so early in the morning, but words fail to describe (as they often do) the fog and the sunrise and the "Transmissions Replaced" at 6AM on The City of New Orleans with my man, my coffee, and mon pays whipping by our dusty windows at seventy miles per hour.

Regardless,

I have been trying to describe the man seated across from me (and what we are to one another) without the words 'partners,' because we are not lawyers, 'lovers' (but not spouses), 'friends,' yes, but fucking vigorously, citizens, but not first class (not really). And all of the fortune tellers, candle-lit and dope sick in Jackson Square have no words for what we are, either, finding fuck-all in their tea leaves (arranged like so many useless cursors) that have long since given up on the question.

Kelly J. Powell

<u>Another Boy Risen</u>
(*for Matthew Shepard, and his family's loss*)

You are yesterday's news now, lovely boy
turned into another Christ figure at your death. But
in life, I see you laughing, a toddler clapping

hands together or touching grass or sand,
grains and leaves running through small fingers, your
first Christmas tree lights twinkling (just for you)

your wonder brighter than any star. We have,
all of us, known joy like that, even if
we cannot remember just now. Your friends

and classmates are older and have lost
love ones, surely as the sun will rise. Forgive them,
they may know better now. Forgive us all.

Anthony Radovich

<u>At 15</u>

In the 70s few things
brought comfort:
a handheld yellow transistor
radio, Paul Lynde, Joanne Worley,
Donna Summer, the streets of Seattle.

I syphoned gas from cars
in Tacoma to get away weekends,
to find other queers, sex workers,
misfits, dyke aunties. We congregated
at Penney's on Second and Pike,
(the first needle exchange site),
we watched out for each other,
turned tricks, slept in bath houses,
the doorman at The Golden Crown
disco, where Queens ruled, sometimes
let us in. Always boys on
Second, women on First—
pride infused—this was our:
Freedom. Risk.
Revolution. Liberation.
Survival.

Fallen Souls

replaced by regimens of
highly active antiretroviral
therapy: the drug cocktail
to stop AIDS, when my medication
stops working I spin into anxiety
I have few options left—at the
mercy of big Pharma my sunny
disposition tested—like when
new KS lesions emerge.

Or when the message was,
get fat don't die? But does
my ass look good in these jeans?

We take our geno and phenotype
tests. I suggest clear focus from
gay men on panels to assist big
Pharma in naming the pills
we take every day. Maraviroc?
Really? Mmmm, sounds sexy,
so butch. And now undetectable
equals un-transmittable. We went
from patient zero to getting to zero

and quintessential gay couples
work together for optimal health.
But I'll see you in the streets.

Spirits Slipping Away

I stopped my list of dead boys at number 58
after John died in 97. Before visiting him, I called
the 3rd floor nurses' station at Bailey Boushay
to check if his family was there.

AIDS left my friend unable to talk or eat,
thrush coated his tongue. He used a small
writing tablet to communicate. I climbed
into his bed and held his frail body,

tears welled in his eyes, I caressed his face,
wiped his mouth; he welcomed my touch,
but he grew agitated so they strapped him
to the bed, put mittens on his hands

prevention to keep the feeding tube intact
with its liquid concoction of sustenance and
medications. After the funeral, at home crying
on the edge of my bed he sat next to me,

but no one was there. I miss how we held
each other, we were lonely and scared.
Is there a dance-floor where you are now?
Are angels' gender-less?

Barb Reynolds

<u>Poem That's Taken 40 Years</u>

I don't know how long I held
that receiver, curly cord
anchoring me in a thick fog
of stun. Details swirl and cloud.

It was one night in eleventh grade.
My mom called out that the phone
was for me. I ran to the kitchen, *Hello*?

LEZ!!!   Click.

I said to myself—or perhaps out loud—
Oh my God, that was Mina. Mina,
my best friend. She stashed
her brace for scoliosis in my room
every morning on her way to school,
we smoked my mom's cigarettes, hated
the world together.

The next morning, standing
at my locker, dreading and dragging,
wondering how she found out,
I felt eyes burning my face, my back.
Friends ignored, or stared
until I looked away. In the bathroom,
I saw my name on the stall wall
in black letters—or were they red—
Barb Reynolds is a LEZ.

I washed my hands, breathed air
into the folds of my lungs,
and began the long walk
through the halls. I perfected
a shell. And it encased me.

<u>Ash</u>

My thoughts are caged in, trapped.
Every day they look out, rattling
the bars, trying to squeeze through—
they drive me crazy.
But, a skilled and careful jailer,
I tossed the key a long time ago.

My mother read my journal
when I was seventeen.
Then she took her pen to it:
We've never had a QUEER
in the family before! Circling
and underlining things.
You're SICK! Drawing arrows, pointing.
You need a psychiatrist!!

I burned it. Every single page
and the cover, too. As if fire
could incinerate her hatred.
Or mine.

For years, I didn't write. And if I did,
it was followed immediately
by such blazing. As if fire
could reduce her words
to ash.

Originally published in Apogee Journal in 2016 as part of their Queer History Folio.

Dennis Rhodes

<u>When</u>

When two men dancing
in public was forbidden –
yes, those were the days!

When a red light flashed
to clear the floor of faggots,
the cops just outside.

When cops thought of men
getting blowjobs in restrooms
beneath their dignity

to even arrest.
When the darkness worked both ways,
hiding awful truths.

When danger was real.
Today's synthetic version
did not yet exist.

When homosexuals
were stealthy mice in the walls
of society,

heard but rarely seen,
their sins and perversities
much feared, but ignored.

When men connecting
for sex was a miracle –
forget about love

which, when it happened
was a grand calamity,
a true gift from God.

Stonewall was nice, but I must say
it took the drama out of being gay.

<u>Sparks</u>

I see two men
up against a wall
just letting sparks fly
(not talking at all);
I feel two hearts
pumped up and ready,
two sets of eyes
holding steady;
I feel vibrations
going awry:
love's a glimmer--
a firefly.
Love loses out.
Silence prevails.
Sex must suffice
when all else fails.

<u>Spiritus, once more</u>

"They don't realize how beautiful they are" –
a wistful comment, a middle-aged friend.
Not true, I thought. I did not want to be
rude so I said nothing, smiling
as if in agreement. They know exactly how
beautiful they are, in just the same way
a hunter will match his gun to his prey
or a photographer adjust his lens
keenly, to the image before him. All
is calculation, cool artful cunning.
The finest artists make it look easy.
The most charming boy in this teeming crowd
is a master of the "spontaneous";
watch him as he chooses a heart to break.
Watch the chosen beg for the privilege.

Steven Riel

<u>The Teacup I Desire</u>

The pattern of teacup I desire
depicts bouquets of mauve roses
tied together by just-picked violets.
Once tea's poured out, a sipping
striptease could reveal thorn
by thorn, as Earl Grey eases
down the length of stem,
at last unveiling unopened buds,
their inviting scents
glazed beneath sugar sediments.

To lift this flowery
vessel in my hands,
to walk it to the cashier, & blushing
or not, to state, *I'd like this,*
would draw a noticeable dot
out where it could be
connected.

        If I begin to collect
teacups (not to mention matching
tea trays, sugar bowls, creamers),
ownership might imply the swan-like
curve in this cup's handle
replicates a sway in my soul,
how I'd arch my arms out of
a thin sweater if I were a starlet
at some Hollywood supper--but naturally
the indelible dots would have proliferated by then,
cups & cups & cups' worth: upside-down tulip skirts
fit for Marie Antoinette & *moi*;
angle-handled Art Decos
in lozenge-like crackle
leaning forward to chat at a café--

Might this step towards
one schoolmarmish cup unlatch all
the knickknacks that polka-dot my mind:
salt & pepper sets of every bent & hue
dishing each other across what-not shelves
lining stairs that spiral turret-high
in my dreams--grasshopper-motif bric-à-brac,
amber brooches, blue Nancy Drews,
buttons like peppermints, scroll-handled keys....

An obedient boy, forbidden his own stuffed animal,
sits on the edge of his sister's bed
when he finds himself alone. Eventually
his sweaty palm pets not the velvet,
but the shadow of her dog--

yes--honeybee heads for the rose it wants,
shoves proboscis into clenched blossoms,
rubs hairy forelegs into pollen
to pack its perfect honeycomb. The gold
splash on my teacup's handle
mirrors me back as a small dot
that's now part of its pattern.

<u>Fingernails</u>

      Each day I fail to trim their advance
   past where a real guy would have
bit them to the quick,
    & their tips nip my palms,
       thumbs & fingers stretch & flex,
         butterflies arching toward
           bangles of sky.

Then danger rises, rises:
   when bulbs sprout wings;
      when pronouns flit through branches
       & wrists take their first flutter;
         when the actor, all antennae,
          blends into the role
           that is his birthright;
             when he finds himself
              with O for a mouth
               needing new words.

What if he ends up a murderess?
   What if all she unfurls
      can't be folded up & put away?

       (The Halloween I wore press-on nails,
         my best friend cooed,
           You've never looked so radiant.
          Defiant, we tottered across
           Manhattan in heels,
         sprayed by scattershot jeers
        from knots of toughs.
       Near some curb
     the glow got lost.)

Week after week,
I clip back my latest millimeters,
flush their ten thin strips down the john;
prune perennials before any ruffles uncurl;

slice off powdery wings
for fear of where I might alight;
never, never letting that What, that Me
    unclench

until what I have become
becomes but this:
no not ever
    a flower taking flight.

<u>Ishmael's Afterthoughts</u>

"But though the picture lies thus tranced..."
Moby Dick, Chapter One

I curl under our covers
after my considerate savage
tucked shut the door on his way downstairs.
Finally at ease, in spite of
this God-forsaken mattress
(*stuffed with seashells*, I joked to myself,
long after Queequeg snuffed out the light),
I absolutely must linger
to face bumpy facts.
Half asleep, I slide my palms
where sheeted lumps still hold
the warmth of his harpooner's frame.
His arm around me & the rise it caused
thrust the answer upon me.
No wonder I jostled, cajoled, roused him
so pointedly, repeatedly, insistently.
Of course I recoiled at first, aroused
by a heathen's unconscious clasp.
Who would simply embrace
a damned identity? But
a mind of my own I've always had,
working out facts to their logical ends.
Methinks my Creator blessed me with this curse.
When the needle of my compass
should be whizzing madly,
I have an anchor, an explanation
for the foul weather icing my soul,
even through April, when my best pupils
thought me God. The architecture
of sailors & their shoulders I ached for unawares,
their massive calves scaling mizzenmasts,
their horsepower torsos sprawled at sunset,
their swearing & snoring & silence--
for these I blackened my name,

walked away from my post
before term's end.

I should have nuzzled, but barely,
against his tattoos at daybreak,
mapped my Pacific paradise.

Like a whale that must sometimes breach, or die,
might this pagan roll beside me
if invited by my eyes? Might there be a signal--
might there be a softness--
might two Polynesian paddlers
sway together in rituals
unimagined by preachers?

And if the same whaler took us both on
to yearn three years
                    across hammocks?

                    Up with me!--
to breakfast, to my bunk-mate's side,
where he points his boots
toward the docks, a destiny without.
There are forbidden things
a quiet man may quietly desire.
I couldn't yet embrace the dream
embracing me at dawn,
but given one more chance, for all the world
I wouldn't break that waking's sacred trance.

<u>New School</u>

Banished: purple pants. Dumpster-stuffed,
along with saddle shoes with two-inch heels.
Heels. When I first came upon the pair of them,
spot-lit within the Thom McAn window for men,
I paused, anxious & transfixed,
two Saturdays in a row, drawn to all that suede
arches of this style suggested
upon a carpeted pedestal.
I sported them the first day
at my first high school.

Couldn't have made a more neon
mistake. As I lowered my gaze to lines
dividing floor tiles, I learned
a face won't burn all the way
from Homeroom to Math class.

St. Jude, thanks for this second school,
second chance to get lost, blend in. Navy-
blue windbreaker, gray cords,
worn Keds. At home I practice
walking like a boy, aligning each step
along parallel tracks. I nest inside
a corner study-carrel, become gerbil
without squeak, scratch,
or telltale patter of scamper.

I shun other slouching misfits even if
at lunch I nibble turkey tetrazzini alone.
Too bad this new school's rules say
even Four-Eyes play sports after two o'clock.
My shins block kicks in third-team soccer.
Muddy, sagging pads almost cushion bone,
& I wonder if I'll always need a burrow.

Unnoticed underclassman
on a locker room bench, I
don't let slip a mammoth moan
when the Varsity MVP strips down (*Good God*)
to just plump cockhead, its scrolled corona--
trophy-winning mousetrap--inches
from my enormous, untamable eyes.

My Perfect Confession

"Bless me, Father, for I have sinned.
This is my first confession ..."
The nuns had drilled us to begin

just so, then list our transgressions
--as if, in that dim closet, each soul could
enter into grace through just one rote expression.

They said--perhaps they misunderstood--
that this was our one chance
to wipe clean all sin staining childhood;

that Father Grady's sidelong glance
through that yellowed, linen screen
stood in for the burning bush, God's lance-

like, all-knowing glare. If God had already seen
what I had done to my dink at night, why
must I now report my secret use of Vaseline?

To whom could I turn to supply
the grown-up words for what we boys had done--
our tingling skin, our silken thighs?

At seven, I'd reached The Age of Reason.
In bed at night, those misdeeds I could wear in public
I'd unpack, unfold, smooth out one by one;

silently rehearse my handpicked
offenses; then re-pack them in piles
tidy as lies. At church, the velvet curtain hung thick

in my hand as I slipped into the box. The tile
floor was no different inside than out. I heard a tap.
A crack of light widened, revealing the profile

of our priest. There was no way out of this trap.
I lied to my Mom. I shot a spitball at our dog Tory.
Then came that pause between a bolt & its thunderclap.

Forallmysins, Iamverysorry.
I waited for God to strike me dead.
I crept to the altar, knelt before our glistening Mary.

I whispered my penance while Jesus' heart bled.
Wouldn't justice, like a second hand, be swift & exact?
No: even breathing slows down when one's full of dread.

At the heavy front door, sunlight pushed me back.
As if sprung from nightmare, I knew with a start
God would let me live, with my guilt intact.

Matthew Roberts

<u>Dismissed</u>

All I see is a boy demonstrating his naivety,
While he boasts of his masculinity.
He preaches of the colors and their meanings, regardless,
Proceeds to lecture me on how to adjust my harness.
Versatile, he claims, is his role,
But he could never mount this, only a pole.
As he mocks a daddy standing in the corner feeling fat,
"Go to the gym if you want to look good in that."
Cockiness defines him while he converses on his tastes in men,
The body types, the genders, nothing below a ten.
If only he knew what I had to do to thrive,
I helped invent those colors, we needed them to survive.
My generation created the harness and its fellow parts,
In my day, a boy with his looks would only serve to break hearts.
The boy should learn to respect his sir, and try to engage,
He will be lucky if he looks as good as that daddy when he is that age.
This new and "improved" generation,
With absolutely no appreciation.
I keep telling myself, 'They don't know of the struggle, or sacrifice.'
They come out like it is a new job offer, no longer a role of the dice.
Personally, I was afraid for everything, especially my life,
Ending up homeless and possibly greeted with a knife.
He makes me furious, as if he is an expert of this scene,
No one would take him seriously, definitely not this queen.
Then I remember, if it weren't for the ones who fought so hard,
He wouldn't be able to enjoy these liberties completely unscarred.
That thought eases my heart and maybe one day he will learn,
If he wants respect, it will have to be earned.
Until then, with a lack of interest in his gaze and a flick of his wrist,
Suddenly it becomes official, I am dismissed.

David and Goliath

Standing on those steps I knew.
I knew we would prevail,

Love would win.

The others disagreed,
All 10,000 of them, against 2 of us.
My boyfriend and me.
Holding hands in unity,
A monumental moment.
David and Goliath proportions,
Ironically lost to the Christian audience.
They shouted their disgust with force,
Casting stones upon us.
Spitting as they walked by,
Cursing obscenities,
Damning us to Hell.
The God I knew,
The God we supposedly share,
Loved me,
Loved US unconditionally.
Many "prayed" for our souls,
They ridiculed my boyfriend and I for being who we are,
I had to believe that love would prevail.

Love would win.

We needed to show them what love was capable of.
One month later,
Inside the building before me, a temple amongst the masses,
The judges would vote.

Love would win!

Thankful

We can adopt!
We can get married!
We should be thankful.
Thankful for the rights that everyone else always had.
Thankful for being late in the game.
Tell me,
What representation do we have in literature?
A single book shelf amongst the masses.
What albums may I choose?
A couple artists hidden in a plethora of actual award winners.
Where are the gay characters in TV and film?
Either background voices,
Or one film every five years.
We should be thankful.
Society says not to be homophobic.
How can it not?
Subconscious conditioning from a lack of variety,
Only causing confusion and shock once revealed.
What else would you expect?
But I am the ungrateful one,
I am missing our strives,
Not giving enough credit.
I should be thankful.
Wouldn't you be?

<u>Lucky</u>

I wasn't looking for tolerance,
I yearned for acceptance.
One never knows the outcome.
The fear exists.
Not knowing if you will have family,
Not knowing if your friends will stay by your side,
Not knowing if you will have a roof over your head.
Each reveal as terrifying as the next.
How do I say it?
How do I stay true to me?
What I knew as love may be no more.
Pop culture only focuses on this moment,
We never know what happens after.
What about the rest of my life?
The unknown is what I yearn for.
I was one of the lucky ones.
My heart aches every moment knowing someone,
Somewhere,
Reliving the same horrid experience,
But their story may be different.
Also yearning for acceptance.
Bravery comes in many forms.
At the extreme,
But not unheard-of,
Coming out could be the difference of life or death.
Keep this in mind if someone tells you their truth.
You will never fully understand,
The fear in their heart.
We have come a long way,
We still have a long way to go.
It only takes one to make the difference.
Will they be as lucky as me?

Rita "Rusty" Rose

<u>Put the 'T First</u>

Lesbian, Gay, Bisexual, and Transgender:
Do you know why this acronym is not correct?
Because the 'T community were some of the first
To fight for freedom at Stonewall!

So, put the 'T first, it is where it belongs!

Musty, smoky, dismal dank hole in the wall—
Reeks of beer, darkness and independence
About to be born.

Put the 'T first, it is where it belongs

Inside; sitting on a stool, purple midriff, black eyeliner—
Trans woman tapping her foot against a squat bar stool

Put the 'T first, it is where it belongs

Queers, Bull daggers, Queens in drag—
Call us what you may we are all here,

Put the 'T first, it is where it belongs

Purple midriff, black eyeliner—beautiful sweet speaking
Woman touches my long red hair…we lift our glasses to cheer

Put the 'T first, it is where it belongs

Jukebox blaring—Jimmy ain't coming back… leader of the pack…
One fine day—could be today!
Purple midriff, eyeliner black, bangs her bangles against the bar,
Tears in her eyes…Somewhere over the rainbow, Judy went!

Put the 'T first, it is where it belongs

Blue-eyed blonde stroking my fancy, dancing slowly; I'm in Heaven
House lights—overhead…grab a guy, any guy!

Put the 'T first, it is where it belongs

Plainclothes on a beat—coming in from the street,
The club was raided for bar owners who would not comply
And when we patrons told the cops to let bygones go by,
With fear in their hearts—guns to the chest
They shouted the words—faggot, poof; you can imagine the rest!

Put the 'T first, it is where it belongs

Purple midriff, Trans woman of fifty, in a nasally voice
She mourns…she warns…JUDY DIED, Judy died…
Hey copper, leave us alone—
Bartender out from behind the bar bounding
Into the darkened hall; cop nipping at his heels.
Face to face—if they were lovers they would
Embrace—but this is not the case,
Young Bull Dagger in a fringed vest runs from the hall
To the bar front shouting "They are going to kill us"

Put the 'T first, it is where it belongs

Purple midriff, eye lined woman jumps to her feet
She leads the cry…enough, leave us alone!
Alone…we are told to sit…some stand…
Too much confusion I cannot understand

Put the 'T first, it is where it belongs

Purple midriff is yanked outside—clutching her hands
On the door as she tries to resist
"Identify," cop shouts ripping at her chest; and they are
Pushing me back, hey man, I am really pissed!
Stone Butch Vinny caught in the shuffle;

Standing strong with purple midriff
As they shout: leave us alone!
Transgender woman cries, Judy died…enough…are we going to die?

Put the 'T first, it is where it belongs

It is all surreal…impulsive happening.
A surprise…S…U…R…P…R…I…S…E --- UPRISE!
Black, White, Latino, Straight…Gay…Old and young…
We take a stand
In unity, we raise our fists
I am not…we are not…going to be harassed any longer!
And, outside the crowd is growing stronger!

Put the 'T first, it is where it belongs

Shouts inside are deafening…leave us alone…let us be!
A burly cop is pushing me…crowd breaking…we are shoved
Out of the door,
Purple midriff, black eyeliner smeared all over the floor!
We are not—I will not take this any longer!

Put the 'T first, it is where it belongs

I take a stand, jump on the man and graze the eye of
'The man' who is
Bashing Trans purple midriff
This could have been you, and you… any one of you… Do you see!

Put the 'T first, it is where it belongs

Transgender woman smiles as I raise her by her hand;
Some flee into the street as my friend
Is protesting again

Put the 'T first, it is where it belongs

Paddy wagon is now in the cobbled street,
Cops dragging purple midriff by her feet,
High heel in hand, and I am on the back of the man
As we all take a stand

Put the 'T first, it is where it belongs

Say it again:

Put the 'T first, it is where it belongs

T-L-G-B and even S for straight, this is how our acronym should be
The night we were all set free
Fighting for freedoms at Stonewall,
I will never forget—beautiful Transgender woman
Of fifty—purple midriff and eye lined,
Long dark hair, her voice raised over the din.
She led the way, this is why I say:

Put the 'T first, it is where it belongs
Again:

Put the 'T first, it is where it belongs

Put the 'T first!

<u>Oscar Wilde</u>

Romantic one; feet on shaky ground
Poetic verses and gentle words have been drowned
Morality whispers sinful 'dare nots'
Imprisoned, is adoration; a societal boycott!
Antagonistically speaking, love is love not to be feared

Tenderhearted playwright in Reading Gaol you rot
Tousled by the love letters written— for you— a poetic garotte
Broken man— two years of tedious labor— sentence for love
Adulation, one does not speak of
Wedged in antiquity are epochs stifled; ideas blear
No longer in cleft rock shall you hide; in valleys weep, or gaze upon stars unclear
For in the name of progress, your tears, we honor you, dear LGBTQ pioneer!

<u>THEY</u>

They are one not two
They are not he or she
Nor me or you
They have identity
Not to be confused or are
They waiting to decide
Their sexuality any time soon
They are they
As she and he
Could be me or you
They are simply they
When greeted by us

<u>South Broome</u>

It is Monday, ten pm; I sit on a black wooden stool in a Lesbian
Bar far away from the nuances and predictabilities of the heterosexual
world.
I am thinking about us—when times were happier.

Our passions are now quashed but I continue to think. My thoughts
keep
Flashing like a constant pressure upon a shutter; a long-playing record
stuck in a groove.
They keep skipping and droning—do you remember when?

I wash down these images with cola. Some taste sugary, some are
bubbly
And some sting the delicate lining of my throat.
Love is oft like that, sweet when it is found; sour as when it has gone
bad,
Bitter as when it is lost…
My visions of you dissipate.

The Indigo Girls blare from a jukebox. They are singing, "There is life
down below me."
I think about the verse as pool sticks and stools are pushed aside.
Couples are hurrying to the already crowded dance floor.

A Stone Butch in a green and white striped shirt saunters towards me
Gently stretching her hand in my direction
She is the reminder of why I am so proud to be the Dyke that I am—
She is proof love exists…

Love—when it finds me, will take me home…
It is Monday, ten pm; I sit on a black wooden stool…

Squeezed a Blood Red

Sunshine State; city beautiful
South Orange Avenue
Squeezed a blood red—

Magical Playland
Where mice scurry and Pixie's sprinkle dust
They bow their animated heads as
The Queen of Hearts sits in a tea cup; sobbing
Her caricature smile upside down
Squeezed a blood red—

Earlier downtown, dance club
Is bustling, vibrant and gay
It is Latino Night on a Saturday
Young hearts, joyous and alive
Mambo, Cha-Cha, free style—
D.J. spinning latest tunes; last tunes
As night is squeezed a blood red—

Madman, mass shooter, massacring
LGBTQ patrons –trapped inside
Our Family— most all in their prime;
Melodic syncopated rhythms still stream
In the club as gun shots hammer out
This is the sound of death
As night is squeezed a blood red—

Shocked and shaken youths
Spill out into the Florida night
Everywhere—everywhere you look
South Streets—Kaley—Esther—
Muriel— outstretch their arms to those within reach
A slaughter happened here, a nocturnal unrest
As night is squeezed a blood red—

It is dawn—a black pall sun reluctantly rises
Sulfuric clouds cloak Pulse Night Club
Latino Night—Orlando, has gone awry
Sorrowful…
Sanguine…
Abandoned…
Silent—
Contiguous streets mourn and weep
As they wrap South Orange in a shroud
And the night is squeezed a blood red.

Marc Rosen

<u>Confession</u>

I confess to spite for a world that earns it.
I confess to refusing to forgive.
I confess to hearing apologies, yet not accepting them.
I confess to reveling in the carnal arts, learning to play the body of man as a passionate amateur rather than a refined virtuoso.
I confess to blaspheming in front of churches during mass for the sake of provoking the Church Ladies.
I confess to taking joy in how fundamentalists take personal offense to my laughter and fun.
I confess to dancing naked under the moonlight, and to finding release soon after.
I confess to doing unprintable things in the bushes. In public. Repeatedly.
I confess that I wish I had done that more times than I actually did.
I confess to flirting when I know there could be no attraction.
I confess to constantly doing too much, too fast, too soon, too suddenly, and yet never enough no matter what.
I confess that I no longer know whether I love or hate myself, or if the answer is some paradoxical combination.
I confess to living myriad lives in one, never showing anybody the full scope or sequence of my self.
I confess that I will live and die alone.
I confess that I regret little, and would undo even less.

<u>Memorial</u>

Everything was calm
We were happy in our ignorance,
Unafraid of life's rigor

Then you swept me up
In your maelstrom
Ripped me from my peace

Your smile powered mine for ages,
And I could crash from that slight frown you'd make
Whenever you disapproved of something I said

I waited to say the words I feared the most
I waited until I knew I meant them, and then it was too late
Should I have said them anyway?

Ever since then, you had that look.
The one that told me I've done wrong by you
The one that said I was a jackass again

Soon after, you left us all
Boarded a train, went out to the end
You never came back

I can apologize for being the cause of that look,
I can apologize for never saying the words that I feared,
But I can't apologize for wanting to say them
Not now, not when you're not here to disapprove

<u>My Irish Rogue</u>

We said we'd meet for coffee,
Something neither of us drinks.

That turned into lunch together,
Hours of talking, walking, flirting,
Teasing, baring our souls.

We both know how far it could go.
We both know you leave at month's end,
My Rogue.

You've given me such happiness,
As we talk and text and hug and kiss.
You make me realize what I should search for,
What qualities in man will complement mine.

We talk of what we both want yet cannot have.
What chemistry and biology dictate is our need,
And what conversation shows would make us both
Stronger and better men.

I wish we had more time.
More time to wander aimlessly together.
More time to share our passions.
More time to merge our lips, breath, and bodies.
More time for me to get to know my dashing Irish Rogue.

Soon, your time here will reach its end.
You'll return to your Emerald Isle,
Whilst I stay here with Paumanok.

Our time together was always but a flash in darkness.
Our paths could only meet for a brief while.

I thus beseech you, my Irish Rogue,
Since we haven't very long,
Let our passions' flames burn their brightest
Ere we be parted by July's dawn.

<u>New Year's at the Bunkhouse</u>

Ten screwdrivers, six hours
My ass shakes all over that wooden floor
As I drink and dance to remember and forget,
All at the same time

I join you, then you, then you
An erotic ritual fueled by trance music that
Gets us all hard and aching

Then I dance away, body still moving of its own will
Following the beat without me.

I switch to water, eat something light,
Pop a button on my button-down shirt,
Bump and grind, alone, with others,
Till the buzz is gone
And only the memory remains

Ten screwdrivers and six hours later, I ask myself:
Why was I here?

<u>Who's the Woman?</u>

I set the Facebook status,
Not telling who just yet.
He isn't quite ready.

Yeah, it's not my usual pace, but it works.

Then you ask, "Who's the woman?"

Who's the woman?

Well, it ain't me, and it ain't him!

You volunteering?
Sorry, we're not looking for a threesome!

Rae Rozman

<u>Untitled</u>

It's summertime
and I like to wear all black
and I like the way your hair sticks to your neck
when you pull weeds in the garden
and I like the way you pick a hydrangea bloom
and put it behind my ear.
Because, you say,
darkness will come back much too soon.

<u>An ode to the queer biology teacher after the suicides of the only out
lesbians in school</u>

She wore cowboy boots to the funeral.
Cowboy boots and a brown floor-length skirt and turquoise.
I remember the turquoise. (Or was it teal?)
At 16, all I knew of the world was that people love and people die
and life isn't eternal but suffering is.
At 16 there wasn't time to make mistakes; it was live and break and
love and mourn.

She wore her hair down to the funeral.
It was blonde and it fell in waves to her shoulders.
She held me close and didn't say a word, but her hair smelled like
lavender.
I was 16 and all I knew of life was that people love and people die
and you do the things they say to do
but still, but still, you blame yourself because you couldn't save them.

And then she showed up in cowboy boots to the funeral.
I was 16, and for a moment, in her arms, I believed
there could be more.

<u>To a woman I love, a year after her brain injury</u>
(For M.)

I still remember how your body lit up a room when you smiled
even though I haven't seen it in months--
not since that night in Baltimore when I held your arm after two
glasses of Chianti
and we walked like lovers along the cobblestones.

And I have written dozens of poems about shattered coffee mugs
even though you've only broken three.
And I have learned to love you in your silences
when there aren't words or they come out sideways or you text me in
the middle of the night to ask for a synonym
because there are finite ways to say I love you
with hands or eyes or color-coded binder clips
that never hold enough of yourself together that you make it through
the day
without feeling like a failure.

And I still remember how you used to walk like you owned the world
when women and men trembled
paying homage to the audacious goddess of your hips.

But you are softer now, your edges dulled
to the moment we stood on your porch and you caught my hand and
stopped me from leaving and said
babe, can you hear the hummingbirds calling you home?
Look into my eyes.
Can you hear me calling you home?

<u>Last night I imagined we'd watch the eclipse together</u>

We would be on the roof
we'd have to be
because the rebel in you still wants to be closer to the stars
even though you lost the words to explain astrophysics
when the moon went out

You'd say *science never ceases to astound me*
and I'd see the dendrites frantically reaching across gaps
to cover places that should not be obscured in shadow

I know the earth turns, and with it,
we place ourselves between
what we see and what we can't.
But maybe, in this fantasy,
in the dark,
you wouldn't feel a need to hide your light.

<u>Untitled</u>

And we flirt
        With confusion
        With impossibility
        With each other
Until our words
                circle
back to safety.

Kareena Rudra

<u>Bricks, Sticks, Stones</u>

Lately, it seems like
We are falling apart
At the seams.
Seeing too many things happening
And not being able to do anything,
But too many bricks were thrown
At Stonewall
For me to be sitting quietly
For me to be doing nothing.
Too many people
Being burned-
People were burned alive
Just so I could survive.
We climbed out of ash,
Out of stone, with broken bones,
With no home,
But we still roam these streets
Like we own them,
We take them by storm
Fighting back with twice the force
We scream, with our voices
Demanding our choices.
No matter how much we are muted,
How much our rights are refuted,
We will be heard.
Even if it's just one word
Slipping through the cracks
Of the walls they built to divide us
No matter how much they tried
To hide us
We will be seen, screaming
The names that deserve fame.
The stories that were shamed.
Harvey Milk, Marsha P Johnson

Alan Turing, Christine Jorgensen
James Baldwin, Bayard Rustin,
You are not forgotten.
We will post your stories
On every wall
Of every building
In every town
If it means you stories get out.
You did not fight for nothing.
You did not die for nothing.
There were too many broken homes
Too many broken people
Too many screams,
Too many teens at home
Wondering if it's even worth it,
For it to all be for nothing.
Even though it seems
Like things are falling apart,
Now is not the time to start
Panicking
Now is the time to join hands
And stand so strong and together
We form a wall
A brick wall
A stone wall
Nothing can destroy
Because this world is broken
And we are the only things
That can keep it together.

<u>Before I Don't Get To;</u>

She said not to go to pride that year.
Shaking in fear, "you can't be here
the year after the Pulse shooting
someone might do something,
I'm just trying to keep you safe."
When did my safe space
become such a dangerous place?
I don't want my queerness
to be the death of me.
I don't want to spend forever in hiding
but it might be what i have to do to survive.
I can't do this for the rest of my life,
sitting in silence,
but I also can't live in violence.
I just want to be
without stones cast upon me.
I'm just trying to beat with my heart
before it starts to stop.
I know it's a lot,
but I wanna dance to it
because they didn't get to,
fall in a trance with it
because they didn't get to,
take a chance on it,
because they didn't get to
take a big stance for it
because they didn't get to.
I wanna do all the things I can do
before I don't get to.
because we live in a reality
where my queerness can get the best of me,
could be the death of me.
Where I go to Disney World for the first time
-the happiest place on earth-
and see two men
molded into punching bags
just for holding hands.

Where 49 people died just to dance.
53 wounded,
darted bullets just to feel their pulse.
An impulse to survive,
just to save their lives.
I don't want my queerness to be the death of me,
but it just might be.
That's the world we live in.

Anna Sago

<u>Untitled</u>

"a stray spark
from a tall woman's cigarette
flicked, falls to the ground
shadows cast around the room,
as music moves them
bodies swaying like trees

the fire's fanned
by molotov cocktails
as smoke spirals above, into the night
venus twinkles as the stars align
brightly burning, the light illuminates
all the places we used to hide

pay the police no mind-
ask no questions, and you'll get no answers-
fight no fights and you'll win no battles.
waging war is never easy,
but as the sun comes up the crowd
swells, screaming at the waves of blue:
pride, power, pride, power..."

Jessica Saldaña

<u>Incorporeals II</u>
for Alex

manic panic
pixie dream
girl dust and
fire in
the whole
of my home

remember when
we made that
pact to never
call anything
human
ever again
especially us
especially other
living things
with dog-like eyes

eye shadow you
with my darkness
and we try to rest
in our free
day-old donuts
walking in the rain
isn't so bad

we incorporeals
think of souls
instead of
species specific
body bags
with names
given by
the Fathers

and yet
to not want the
full thing
but to still want
a part of it

apartment music
CA's voice saying
fucking faggot
it's me it's me
I'm the faggot boy
gag me with a spoon
Haha
Hashtag I forgot
what I was saying
when I wrote
this spiral

I light this candle on my alter
for all the things who've died
and will die
for all the terms
time has given us
for all the conditions

oh to be in
New York with
no money
no clout
and no therapist
oh no

I could never think fully enough
thankfully
I have you
to stay here all day and
drink tea
and take a read day

<u>Love Poem</u>

to be brave
enough to
bottom

even though
I've carved
a space
at the top

Sarah Sarai

<u>The Pink Yonder</u>

      some of us pining to meet
state-of-the-art girls
      almighty love
      ever-expansive dewdrop rainbow

other hippie chick handles

      mint-condition girls
      playing their hand

        shuffling a deck
hid up their sleeve of many cards

girls loose with freedoms
      the ones in the gift bag
      yielded to us when we were
      sprung from our jail cell

you know the one.

did Judee know I was queer?

<u>Peril #52 of Having a Mother</u>

Alois talked up
fastidious habits he
observed while engaged
in love's excitations.
Bus drivers on Haight
were clued in, shop clerks,
everyone in a radius knew
his pride of ownership.

I wish Mom talked sex
as much as he did.
I know lots about travels of the spirit.
I'm sort of mental.

May I take off my clothes.
That's a prayer.
May I take off my clothes,
roll about and know the cloud of unknowing.
Sweetie, it wants to be known, don't you think?

Relive those parties where every bottle was uncorked and
passed around and everyone smoked everything, double-
checked each auto's glove box for at least a Sherman or
a roach. And you left with exactly the wrong woman who
was exactly the right one, if only for less than twelve hours.
And not everyone was anything, not white, employed,
focused. And all had self-righteous halos of wild hair
imperfect as a precisely imprecise stitch in a Persian rug.
You had fun. We all did. It had become more possible.

Paula Sayword

<u>Provincetown Remembered</u>

She was walking crowded
Commercial Street on a July afternoon,
wearing cut-off corduroy jeans,
tank top, lace-up work boots,
skin tanned to perfection.
She had nowhere to go, no one to be.
It was before she cut her hair,
still hand rolled her cigarettes,
tough dyke who slept with all her friends.
The street was full of tourists,
moms and dads, kids sauntering behind,
eating ice cream, slices of pizza,
watching half-dressed gay boys
kissing at the corner,
drag queens on roller skates
flying down toward the wharf.
The fishing boats were coming in
with their daily catch of blues and sea bass,
flounder and lobster.
Wind blew in off the Bay,
rigging creaked and clanked,
competing with the voices of men hollering
as they off-loaded their fish,
joking about beer and sex,
the fireworks later that night.
She sat on a bench,
squinted into the sea light,
closed her eyes
and listened to the clanking, the voices,
the boats rubbing against the dock.
Music started playing in a bar up the beach
and she could just make out
a disco beat on the wind,
knew after the fireworks were finished

she would do down the alley to that bar,
drink a few beers,
dance with strange and beautiful women
to the music of Donna Summer,
get hot and sweaty
and stand out on the deck
under a cool mesh of stars,
the tide coming in salty and brave,
the tide coming in.

Walk Toward Myself

I touched a woman for the first time
on a day like this. Mid October.
The meadow behind her New Salem
house breathed with the rise and fall
of Monarch butterflies beginning
their migration to Mexico.
I was stunned by their brave beauty,
stunned by the softness of her breasts,
as we lay together, the afternoon light
drinking down the day.

I was not thinking about marriage
or my husband, a damaged
stoned-out victim of Southeast Asia—
the man at home with our young son.
I was listening to her read Anais Nin aloud
and watching the shadow of dying leaves
waltz on her bedroom ceiling,
knowing in a sharp, aching moment
that my life would never be the same.

On a hungry road with no map, I saw
a dappled mare standing alone on a hill.
I called to her in the shivering half-light of October.
She came to me, nuzzled my face.
I lay down my old clothes, stood naked,
pulled on a tunic and trousers the color of blood,
slipped into worn leather boots, mounted that horse.
The sky was full of nothing but blue.

<u>Outlaw</u>
> *after reading Lise Weil*

She's waiting for the storm,
watches sky darken to pewter,
clouds riding on top of each other.
Thunder grumbling north and west.
She remembers the dappled mare,
the one she rode across a field wide as sky.
An outlaw in trousers the color of blood.
Free. Frightened. Full of lust.
Lust for self, for women,
for the arch of her lover's back.
She was young then,
they all were.
Dreaming of a new nation,
language all their own.
She wants to be an outlaw again,
as if it were forty years ago
before acceptance,
the consequences of inclusion.
Always on edge, excited, pained,
riding across an unmapped landscape.
Hair flying. Breasts throbbing.
Riding that dappled mare.
Storm in her belly.
Thunder between her thighs.

Lois Shearing

<u>Wrong</u>

I knew it, I think,
The first time I watched a girl blink
And my desire to dance as a kid
Came cha-cha-ing up through my hips
To my lips, and out my fingertips
And that well inside me made sense
Like the stars had fallen into alignment
And I knew I was bisexual, long before I knew what that word meant.

Because I love lovers with bodies like my own
I like tongues that taste of languages I've never known
And across those mountains of flesh & bone
It's in the lashes, I always find a home.

Lashes are lashes regardless of gender
They hold back worlds and dare me to enter
I love the way she says my name
And I love the boys who can't look at me on the train
And I've loved up and down a spectrum as endless as rain

But I was made to feel ashamed for so long.
So you tell me, which of these is wrong?

<u>Queer</u>

Learn to hide everything
Even the innocent parts
They love you in theory
But say the practice is an art
They gaze as they stroll by at
You, pinned under glass
One warm day in April
Arms around waists like
Sun kissed skin
They love with more patience
Than any man and wife you've known
You were so loud-mouthed in naivety
But quiet now in your silent fear
Isn't that
Queer.

<u>August in Finbury Park</u>

The ground moves subtly as the tube passes under us
It's mid-August in Finsbury Park and our optimism
is keeping us warmer than the exposed sun
You're laying casually on my lap, and I'm annoyed, I think
You won't let me lay on you
My bare legs are tired and surely it's my turn now?
Your hair and the grass brush against my thighs as
Somewhere far away, our flatmate explains something neither of us
understand
Instead, I admire every pore on your illuminated face
Your chocolate brown hair, the marks where your glasses sit
Between us, the spoils of a punnet melt as flies roam
indecisively between them and our salt-kissed skin
None of us will admit we're getting cold.

By the time we've walked home, the street lamps are on
And that night you let me fall asleep on your chest

Deborah Chava Singer

<u>I Don't Stop Being Bisexual When…</u>

I don't stop being what I am
if I hide it for your comfort
that does not make my life easier
I am not choosing a harder path
but demanding an honest one
I don't stop being what I am
if you take away
my rights, my dignity
I don't stop being what I am
because I'm dating or not
with this gender or that
I don't stop being what I am
because yet again you forgot
or you tell me I'm confused
or greedy
or nonexistent
or afraid to come out all the way
when I'm saying it plain
over and over
despite all the shit
I'm bisexual
no, you can't watch
no, I'm not giving you
an up-to-date sexual resume
or a percentage breakdown
I'm a bisexual
not your weather report
fifty percent attracted to [blank]
with a fifty percent chance of rain
and this word
this label
my twenty-year fuck you
to everyone making us invisible
is not my embrace

of an out-dated gender binary
but my long-held defiant
long-stretched spanning
across more than one community
my claim to overlap space
queer and "straight"
to take my place
on this planet
to recognize
I deserve respect
as a human being
who happens to be something ...
that I won't stop being
no matter what you do
or think,
or forget,
or say
because for me it's a life-long phase
I'm bisexual

<u>To Be Kicked to the Ground and Get Back Up</u>

to work your spirit raw
to stretch, strain, and sacrifice
to the last shreds of your will
and watch the fruit of that labor
fall and rot
to be kicked to the ground
and get back up
and still dare to fall in love
reaching out your hands
no matter the pain
stripped down to essence
then deciding to gather your ashes
and start over
building with wreckage
dancing with baggage
to be kicked to the ground
and get back up
again and again and again
G-d bless the freaks
hooray for the stubborn salvaged
the defiant damaged
the willful unwanted
the beautiful difficult bitches
with their scars and broken-in knowledge
to be rejected and still hold out your heart to share
to be kicked to the ground
and get back up
well nevermind the winners
to lose and yet still try again
savor that victory
and carry it on

<u>And Even This Doesn't Cover It</u>

when I was about fifteen I concluded
no matter how hard I try, I will not be normal
so I should just stop
embrace abnormality
statistical eccentricity
I am a standard deviation
and seriously, I'm not trying to be
and yet some words describe me
more and less
here the offer of identity
a home in family
group-hug community
find a place in safe space
until you slip the wrong phrase
let loose a disliked truth
"you're into that too"
"you like them too"
well that won't do
it took me a long time to appreciate the term fence-sitter
not as something to be called
yeah that still annoys
but as a descriptive of a state of being
straddling, balancing
and not quite fitting
sooner or later reminded
always, sooner or later reminded
they'd rather I not talk about that part of my life
that part of who I am
half straight
half gay
half patient
half praise
half love
half bitch
half mess
half of enough
all me

out twenty years and the improvements are ringing
and yet the hurts still slinging, still stinging
yeah, I should be making my mind up any day now
come out all the way
or get over this phase
which way to go - I'll let you know
maybe I'll pick next decade
probably not
and every uneasy fit in a quest for self-definition
every discovered inherent contradiction
each label with an asterisk
and likely associated judgment
self-ownership with necessitated explanation
and even that doesn't cover it
queer bisexual pansexual poly femme
queer I like the term I would, I'm weird
bisexual we do exist
for real
no, for real
no, you can't watch
pansexual if people know what it means
usually I leave it a silent parenthetical
polyamorous
I used to immediately have to add non-monogamous
now at least people know what it means
okay, now at least people think they know what it means
at least people have heard of it before
now at least people have heard the word before
except for when they haven't
femme
a femme
how is one a femme
a down to earth
skirt-wearing
slightly lazy femme
a wear make-up only when I feel like -
and I'm not allergic to it femme
how is one a femme when most make-up burns your eyes
how is one a femme when your hair is falling out

it aches so bad you don't want to leave the house
and you muster
and strangers still compliment your long mane
they don't know it's getting thinner every day
unlike your body
unlike the fat your doctors routinely struggle to see past to help you
bestowing wisdom like Œno matter how much you exercise -
if you are still overweight it's not enough
voluptuous femme
plus size femme
pay ten dollars extra for clothes in your size then
and be grateful you even have that option
how is one a femme with wide-width feet and wide calves
but about an inch or two wider than most "wide calf" boots wide
calves
and how does one buy cute shoes
as a non-leather wearing, wide-footed femme
when everyone thinks vegetarian equals skinny
because I've been veg longer than I've been out
fat vegetarians are like bisexual men, climate change, and evolution
we really do exist
and how does one get non-leather kinky
with wrists and ankles that are non-skinny
most of the kinky cuffs won't reach
it's actually easier buying shoes
and how does one connect, does one commune
when community, when the world is increasingly
in a space you can't get to
can't get on with the social sharing hashtag
when your tendons and tunnels are wrecked
and it hurts to go online to check, in or out
when it's beyond just wear some special gloves bad
and more like can barely work, can barely even care for yourself bad
and how do you show your pride
for your community that still smokes at rates so high
and you are allergic
too allergic to easily attend a parade
you'd feel left out
again and again

the cycle
all hurt sad mad
so strange this thing
being reminded you are forgotten
all hurt sad mad
yeah, you'd be angry too
you'd have something to say too
all hurt sad mad speak
you'd find a way
all hurt sad mad speak, again
you'd learn to write with your left arm while you ice your right
until it's time to ice that left one too
pushed so long hard wore that left wrong through
because you're that stubborn
because I'm that stubborn
because I'm that
stubborn, difficult, queer
bisexual pansexual polyamorous femme
cisgender female, repetitively damaged
cumulatively strained shy leo freak
with leo rising and my moon in capricorn
and my mess in lukewarm
delicate, bold, fragile, strong
and then some
jew-wiccan, fat vegetarian
kinkish, gothish, earthy, bittersweet bitch
and a complicated wreck
and a lot more
and definitely not shutting up any time soon
definitely not shutting up any time soon

Heather Stewart

<u>Instability</u>

But which do you prefer?
This is just a phase
Are you really gay?
This is just a phase
You aren't gay enough.
This is just a phase

Can I bring her home?
This is just a phase
Is he welcome here?
This is just a phase
What does it even mean to be "queer?"
This is just a phase

My identity, my desires
I am told
They are just a phase
This life,
Of mine,
a phase

Unstable as it is,
a fleeting, shifting phase,
I hold it close.
This life
Of mine
This phase

<u>Stonewall Inn, January 2019</u>

three enter the room to the sound of
"welcome to the Stonewall, bitches"
uttered through darkly lined red lips quickly
moving below a refined smoky eye
lid sparkling with
      glitter

our first time

seated on a
      leather
couch, holding
a strong hand
attached to a
masculine body
      my love

a soft head rests
upon my shoulder
on the other side
attached to a
feminine body
      queer friendship

is physical at times
      embodied
blurry and messy
but without confusion
and without
      fear
         and
filled with
            love.

we are
      safe
here

much has changed

we toast to those before
who made us safe
by their
          courage
                    and
by their
                      sacrifice.

unified across time
we are home

though we have never been
before
and may never return
again

for us,
Stonewall is home.

F Cade Swanson

<u>The Virus You Gave Me</u>

The virus you gave me
Which I thought might kill me
Was delivered with such care and kindness
That it was hard to determine if you
were giving me life,
replacing my sadness with love
Or giving me death
And replacing my sadness with fear.

Either way
I know you were afraid to be alone.
And while giving me your virus connected us
Forever
It also destroyed us.
And we're left with just the virus.
To remind us how connected we once were.

Seth Walker

<u>Bear Call</u>

This is for the bears.
The big & hairy,
so manly we fuck other men!

Who's vetting process is a wrestling match;
if you can't beat me,
you can't bone me.

I need a manly man;
send me a bareknuckle boxing lumberjack on a Harley,
an MMA cage fighting leather daddy wielding a battle axe.

Send me a Russian accent, swearing sailors pink.
Threaten me in German...
yeah...talk dirty to me...

Let's throw each other around the living room,
break shit, then fuck on it...
when the cops show up to our battlefield of man-love...

...let us explain to the neighbors... patiently...
that sometimes, when a man loves another man
very much... ... look.... Just don't call the police anymore...

Give me a grizzly, a grunter,
a switch-hitting, power something,
with no gag reflex.

I wanna hit that with a baseball bat,
cock slap your ass crack,
then barbeque a whole elk for dinner...

I want fisticuffs in my foreplay,
beer & construction all day,

truck stop role-play...

hairy faced fur-papas
giving dome like a metronome;
I need a throat soldier.

I need a creative sadist &
more toys than batman;
with stories not appropriate for pixar.

I want a paddle master, a guitar hero;
give me a metal head who deep grinds to Metallica in a sweaty trailer.
Let's butt-sex to Rob Zombie, flog our dolphins to Flogging Molly.

This is my bear call; come get a piece.
Let's drink fight, fuck &
call it a romantic evening.

If you're "OH" & "OH SHIT" face are the same,
let's sword fight with our meat pipes
until we burst a vein.

Pretend I'm a dust bunny hiding in the closet &
you're just the vacuum to suck me out of it.
They say that the only things to come from Texas are steers & queers...

... & though I do have antlers... hanging on my living room wall...
the bear skin rug lying beneath it,
is where I plan on fucking you first...

So are you gonna keep talkin' shit...
or are you gonna put em up...
& get sexy...

<u>Us Shattered Mirror</u>

The evolution is being
broadcasted in the reflections of our offspring.
The definition of "cool" is changing.

To the terrified children hidden
inside all us independent thinkers:
hold strong...

The dark can be comforting
as a blanket
if you let it.

So soothing
you stop
caring

about the monsters
you've heard rumors of
but never been bitten by.

What's funny about monsters;
they don't play
with their food.

If they had hunger
enough to devour you
you'd be dressed in ether by now.

If it hasn't killed you yet,
seek to understand the power
you already have over it.

This life is two fists full of fireworks &
eyes that set fire to everything
they see.

Self-mastery is no longer an option;
enlightenment is the pendulum swing reaction to the nuclear age.

My fellow earthlings, let us realize
for us, Humans, to believe we
are the most intelligent beings in this universe...

is for gold fish to think people outside the bowl
are things they'll have to wait & ask God about
when they all get to heaven.

It is time we recognize our similarities:
we have all been wrong
about a few things.

We've all been outcasted by the
apartheid walls we all
call your rib cage.

We all know
there are things in this world
we all claim to know,

that we secretly know...
may not be real...
& that's okay...

Down here
in this thing we all call life,
every day you don't die has been lived "successfully",

but are you using your
"not dead yet time" wisely?
Who owns your "right now"?

If you're not enjoying being down here,
why did you choose to
come down here in the first place?
This world is too precious to waste.

It is a sacred space
we've collectively created

for learning as children;
making love like
cannibals after a hunger strike;

dying: heroes, saints, dumpster-hookers
poets & paupers.
(sometimes the last two come simultaneously)

All within one century or less...
Wrap it up in sunsets &
this world is a gift

from our imaginations & nightmares
to those still stuck
on this side of the veil.

This is claymation responding
to our pencil sketching;
sculptures of a painting we all constantly doodle.

It is our shadow reaching up from the concrete
pulling our clenching hands into the ice waters of darkness,
through the ground we use to call stable,

to learn
to love
every part of our self;

even the shadows
we carry
all day long.

Yeah,
this world is one
crazy fucked up place;

but that's why people
like you & me...
we fit in here.

Us poor broken shards....
Us shattered mirror....
knocked off our vanity, in the darkness of the great night...

We are all lonely
for wholeness,
reaching for each other

with hateful blaming fingers,
while the culprit of this predicament disappears
with the stilling of the wind.

Light Stutters

But then there's always one more day...
Wishing the sun good morning,
fondly farewelling stars,
avoiding the non-productivity of sleep
with the excuse of art.

soon dreams will spin creations of their own.
The subconscious storyteller in hiding
will graffiti my eye lids
faster than I'll be able to catch
the discontinuity of.

I will meet another master
who will sit me down
through another lecture
which I will have forgotten most of
by morning coffee.

But I will remember how to vibrate,
how to see through my eyelids
when they are closed,
what conscious light sounds like,
how to catch a hint from my future entangled self.

There will always be another mourning;
another loss of constellations to guide us,
a new day star to blind us,
another thing to fear
offered in place of a thing to do.

Another dream,
another crack in the wall
another idea of freedom seeping into the deep waters
of the collective consciousness
unconsciously.

The dream is
changing.
We, the figments,
will evolve,
fitting the new environment;
evolution is not an opt-out kind of thing...

Tomorrow...
when the sun glazes your face with new day,
breath in the acceptance
that you are in a constant state of becoming & it's okay.

Yesterday is only a marker to prove how far you've come.
Tomorrow is indescribable,
even to the poet,
for it has never happened before in all of history.

It could be the end...
or the beginning...

<u>#8: The Only Thing</u>

The only thing I hate more than you... is me...
for falling this deep...
for walking into such obvious bear traps...
for sticking my heart
where my dick should have gone.

Mark Ward

<u>The "No" Campaign</u>
regarding the Referendum on Same-Sex Marriage in Ireland, 2015.

You try to side-line our voice.
Each choice to exercise free speech
is vilified as irrelevant noise
or worse, as bullying.
The privileged now do their culling
with words, with accusations.
They cry sacrilege, or victim;
our disrespectful arguments hurt them,
bruise them worse than fists flung
by a gurning gang shouting homo,
wound them worse than wedding cakes
baked into hot potatoes.
Those who say No have it much worse.
Their unadorned words entreat no sympathy
so they gussy them up with sophistry;
arguments designed only for the aftertaste.
Just thirty more days until the referendum -
a million more ways for them to run us down,
our resolve picked at by inconsistencies,
by off-topic assertions, by outright fallacies.
Those without an argument can only breed fear.
Just thirty more days until we're in the clear, I hope,
because I won't imagine a world ruled by a no
that's no longer theirs but the whole country's.
I have to believe that this will pass, you see,
that this time will only last as a footnote,
that their voices will recede into the shadows
But you're not letting us speak – that's true
but you're forgetting this poem isn't a space for you,
it's for me, for my friends and family,
those being discussed and dissected by you,
those who are disgusted by the invective you spew,
who can't believe our lives are in the hands of you -

but that's not quite true, is it?
For every lie you slide under the skin,
for all the false claims in your empty fist,
the truth will shine as bright as a lighthouse
overpowering your attempts at myth.

Julene Tripp Weaver

<u>Stonewall</u>

I still mourn Judy Garland
with the queers at Stonewall—
I was one of the flamboyant ones
who'd had enough. Salt-sweat
mascara running my face
getting on with my grief for
my girl. Cop raid ire-fire
this is my right, my life,
you bet I snapped.
Don't push us
when we mourn.

Judy Garland (June 10, 1922 – June 22, 1969)

~Published online at *Qarrtsiluni*, 2010
~Published in *truth be bold—Serenading Life & Death in the Age of AIDS*, Finishing Line Press, 2017

<u>Larks</u>

All the beautiful gay young men—
piano appassionato
glamorous
>   their manhood bent
>   betrayed this life
>   outcasts to continuance
>   their bootless sobs

>   Larks—they sang
cruising this inner passage

On my path the weather has been
grey
>   adaptive survivor
>   (yet) it is you, each Lark, who made my life
>   easier
>   difficult trip into
>   tolerable adventure

to touch such life
in the shadows at the gay disco
dancing with you in your glory

Published in *truth be bold—Serenading Life & Death in the Age of AIDS*, Finishing Line Press, 2017

<u>Sex Pays</u>

I.

Not some mean son
out of the wood shack
carrying his axe to slash
me down—some cunt
bitch, full of, you think
you can write, or some
roller blade dare devil
knocking me out mid-
way round the track
for fun. Not these
blow-for-blow hard
muscle-AP-bullies,
billy clubs in their hands
sneer-faces distorted
mirror fun house
cadavers, tired, years
away from their art
with poisonous snake
tongues. No, give me
someone kind, orange
juice in their hand, a
pink terry cloth robe,
sugar coated words
without harm. Let me
feel such love, true
inspiration bred from
kindness, a kindred soul.

II.

What is true revelation in the story? Is it sex
pays or is it earning that first wad of cash?
It is sex pays. That a girl has a body to fall
back on, like the gay boy street hustler
kicked out of his home. Sex, a way to

earn. In it you may find a minute of kindness
or be fucked-over so bad your body is found
in a garbage can in an alley, a discarded
torso from one bad trick. Sex pays is
the point, some win, others lose.

Published in the Inaugural issue of *Menacing Hedge*, Summer 2011
Published in *truth be bold—Serenading Life & Death in the Age of AIDS*, Finishing
Line Press, 2017

80s Disco Night

Out with the boys at the gay bar sniffing
poppers, we dance a wave with the music

In the ladies' room staggered against the wall
a short Native woman with long hair
catches my eye   her collar bone
glimmers   turquoise on a chain

she slithers into my full frame
plants her lips   against mine
our tongues intertwine   snakes
weave   like a dream

she enters me with a long kiss
we don't notice   when the stall
empties,   we dance our tongues
till she pulls away, with a question,
Who do you have waiting at home?

Well, yeah, I have a girlfriend.
Fuck, she swears and enters
the stall   stunned I stand
seared by her scarlet lipstick

Published in *Riverbabble*, Winter Solstice Issue 34, 2019.

<u>Shoe Watch</u>

Bones grow crooked twisted in heels, spiny threatened ankles
push over on the street, in stilettos she dares to wear
despite doctor warnings, in spite of stares and glares.
Hot pink with bouffant hair sprayed to the sky, we watch

she stumbles against a green light through traffic, cars toot
whistlers hoot wolf calls, she maintains her rigor,
reaches the other side, friends with boa feather scarves
wave her onward to their safe society, enfold her with hugs.

Rick Allen Wilson

<u>Oklahoma, 1969</u>

On June 22, 1969, Judy Garland died.
I heard it on our black and white tv
in our living room in Oklahoma.

I was seven.

"An overdose," my Dad said.
"She took drugs; pills; she was on dope;
God knows what else."

I could not believe the girl
who sang the most beautiful
song in the world about hope
in a place beyond the rainbow
had gone to sleep with barbiturates
and forgot to set the alarm clock.

I grieved. I conducted a private funeral
in my bedroom with the door closed.
I sang, "Somewhere Over the Rainbow."
I was a gay kid in Oklahoma.

I did not know, when I was seven,
that, a week later,
friends and lovers and brothers and sisters,
my tribes, my people,
in a bar in Sheridan Square
in Greenwich Village
were also grieving
the night our Judy was laid to rest.

And so the story goes . . .

That night was different
from all other nights nights—
something happened:
some crack in the rainbow,
a break in the lining that separates
earth from heaven,
heaven from earth.

But God, that night, set His bow
in the heavens once more:
an afterthought, a divine edit
to a promise He once made
to an inexperienced ship's captain
some years before the Internet:

"And let it be known," God amended.
"This shit is done.
No more shall Sodom and Gomorrah burn.
And what was that Lot *thinking*,
offering a mob of rapists his daughters?
#ThemToo, but I digress."

And God saw those cocktails,
made with love and anger and rage,
by and for those drag sisters
and lesbians of America,
and God said, "*Damn, that is good!*"

As they fought back in Greenwich Village,
someone, I hope, I believe, I know,
was fighting for a seven-year-old
in Oklahoma or Nebraska or Wyoming or Arizona,
self-defining as odd, weird, different, wrong,
and inexplicably inadequate.

I think of who I was at seven
and a dress my grandmother
let me wear as I played on her carport:
white gathered, tufted chiffon with occasional

sequins to catch the light:
black and blue, like jewels
bursting from the red Oklahoma dirt.

On the night of Stonewall,
I hope someone was wearing
something white with sequins.

And I hope she took off a shoe
and wielded it like a hammer
the way I once saw my granny
hold a hammer outstretched
above her head
showing she meant business
to an assailant
threatening to deface
her own book of morality.

But then again, that same granny
took on would-be avengers
who showed up in the night
with a baseball bat
blood-lusting for retribution on my uncle—
that granny jumped a white thug's back,
grabbed two fistfuls of his hair,
and rode him with fury like he was a bull
of the Old West.

Grannies, you know, are the grandmothers
and patron saints of drag queens.

<u>Sheridan Square, 1992</u>

I went not to Stonewall,
but a few doors down,
to The Duplex—
now the old *Rose's Turn Duplex*
that became a beacon
of gentrification,
the one which looks like
dressing room mirrors,
its large white bulbs
mystically calling you inside
to come sing a song
and drink seventeen
precursors to Cosmos
and join with the lost boys and girls
as we soar with Peter Pan.

I was with a friend
and drank too much
and kept staring at
a beautiful, entitled
hunky Frat Boy. He seemed
out of place, out of tribe,
but had two strange friends with him,
both looking to him for approval.

I assumed, because he was there,
he, like me, was gay.
I had journeyed from Oklahoma
to the Emerald City
along the Yellow Brick Road
to The Duplex near Stonewall.

It was winter
and I was an actor
and I was broke.

My friend and I were hammered.
Done with The Duplex,
acknowledging *That love is rare
and life is strange. Nothing lasts,
and people change,* *
but we were kind of Done
with some Egos
and wanted a change of scenery.

We threw back a couple more
on stools at Stonewall.
My friend mentioned
we were *at* Stonewall,
the Stonewall.
I was unimpressed,
my mind still on Frat Boy.
I sat there not knowing:
I was the entitled one.

As we braced against the cold
and passed The Duplex once again,
Frat Boy and his minions
were on the corner.

Frat Boy and I locked eyes
and I was so drunk
that when we gazed
and saw each other
and knew each other
and wanted each other
in that gaze, I giggled to my friend,
loudly enough that
Frat Boy could hear,
"My God! He's following me!"

And Frat Boy, flanked
by Eddie Haskell and Biff Tannen
said menacingly,
"Hey, faggot. How's it going?"

And there was a sudden chill,
heavy, dangerous, and cold,
not a hundred feet from Stonewall.
I put my head down and kept walking.
The Joy of the Evening was Done.

I did not know until then
what he was doing
in The Duplex that night,
a warrior without his lacrosse stick,
or boxer without his bag,
from Dartmouth or Princeton
or the Upper East Side.

But in the shadows of Stonewall,
he lived his myth: he was arrogant,
entitled, powerful, cocky, straight,
maybe even curious,
but he was not, that night,
with Haskell and Tannen at his sides,
what our foresisters fought *for*.

All the way back to Queens that night,
I looked over my shoulder
on the 7 under the East River
and on the sidewalks of
Jackson Heights.

I'm still looking for him
thirty years later.

* From *Getting My Act Together and Taking It On the Road*
by Nancy Ford and Gretchen Cryer

Parade Route to Sheridan Square, 2015

We are dressed in pink
and white
atop a wedding cake.
A white arch frames us
as we kiss for the crowds
repeatedly
along the route.

We are the celebrants
but Andromeda is the idol.
On the flatbed dance floor
she owns the day.
Supplicants in pink and white
sleeveless tuxedo t-shirts
grind in victory and praise
with the goddess'
blessing of renewal.

I am here with my husband
and my in-laws beside me
showing the world we can stand
on fabulous cakes together
renewing prior promises.
Our wedding party of friends marches the sides:
mostly proud, straight Millennials
knowing the place to be
at Pride is most certainly *in* Pride.

As we approach Edie Windsor
the plan goes awry:
the four of us race through the vows,
omitting three or four
so we can get the kiss right
(Edie is already standing)
as we and the Grand Marshall
grandstand align.
Toward the end of the parade

before the magic ends
in a parking lot,
(which is across town and
not over the rainbow),
two streets converge.

I was romantically lost
in the day,
intoxicated with the love
of my husband and his parents,
with tens of thousands cheering us:
neighbors who came to wave,
former students who jumped and screamed,
and messaged through social media;
strangers, who smiled a moment,
at a mom, dad, their son, and son-in-law.

As the streets came together,
I saw Stonewall suddenly in view.
From atop the wedding cake,
my heart sent out
a soul-kiss of gratitude
for all that ever happened
from the refusal of 1969,
the celebrations of 1976,
the losses to AIDS in the 1980's
and beyond;
all that was enabling me
to be a proud groom, once again,
for a moment in time
alive and happy on a day in June.*

Somewhere, the toe-headed kid
from the clay of Oklahoma
still dances the carport in
his grandmother's white dress
with the blue, and black sequins.

* with thanks to Virginia Woolf and Michael Cunningham

Daniel Jerzy Zyzniewski

<u>Call Me by Your Cry</u>
(dedicated to James Ivory)

I
In pain of feelings
we create a new language -
                    - circulation in our faces
questions and answers -
                    - under the skin strategies of protection
invisibility emerged from experiences
imprints dancing in heartbeats rhythm
we know what to do staying in front of danger
when yearning explodes through
our body expression in salvation

II
Call me by your cry
and I'll call you by mine
going down with your tears
we'll fly to happiness
above the Earth on wings of my faith
in your sensibility and tenderest sense

Standing with past behind us
in present as a step to the future
we'll keep together our hearts
creating new signature

Call me by suffer in silence
and I'll call you at the same time
feeling better a resilience
of every moment in love-by

About The Authors

Joel Allegretti is the author of, most recently, *Platypus* (NYQ Books, 2017), a collection of poems, prose, and performance texts, and *Our Dolphin* (Thrice Publishing, 2016), a novella. His second book of poems, *Father Silicon* (The Poet's Press, 2006), was selected by *The Kansas City Star* as one of 100 Noteworthy Books of 2006. He is the editor of *Rabbit Ears: TV Poems* (NYQ Books, 2015), the first anthology of poetry about the mass medium.

Rachel Antrobus is a bisexual woman from England, currently living in Switzerland working as an au pair.

Con Artist's legal name is, in fact, **Con Artist**. She has a BS in Fine Art and works with various mediums involving visual and performance art, such as painting, sculpture, singing, and dancing. At present, she's currently working on a show for Broadway with *Stonewall's Legacy* coeditor Rusty Rose, titled "NoConintended".

Elliot Ayres is a transgender, Asian American man who lives and works in Washington, DC. He grew up in the DC area and recently graduated from the College of William & Mary, where he started to transition in his senior year.

Ellen Bass's most recent book is *Like a Beggar* (Copper Canyon Press, 2014). Her poems appear frequently in *The New Yorker* and *The American Poetry Review*. A Chancellor of the Academy of American Poets, she teaches in the MFA program at Pacific University. ellenbass.com

In her writing, **Sally Bellerose** loves to mess with rhythm, rhyme, and awkward emotion. Bellerose writes about class, sex, illness, absurdity, and lately, growing old.

Her novel *The Girls Club* won many awards including an NEA Fellowship. Her poetry is featured in *Lady Business*.

Raymond Berry is a native Chicagoan and poet. His works appears in *Reverie, To Be Left With the Body, Spaces Between Us, Warpland, City Brink, The HIV Here & Now Project, Cactus Heart, Assaracus*, and the forthcoming anthology by Belt Publishing, *Chicago Neighborhood Guidebook*.

Michael Gray Bulla is a gay, transgender man from Franklin, Tennessee. He was the 2017 Nashville Youth Poet Laureate, and *I Go To The Movies With A Boy* and *To The Girls Who They Say Converted Me* are both published in his debut poetry collection, *LETTERS TO THE HOME*. You can find him on Twitter under @graybulla.

Guillermo Filice Castro is a poet, photographer and translator. He's the author of the chapbooks *Mixtape For A War* (Seven Kitchens Press) and *Agua, Fuego* (Finishing Line Press). His work is featured in *Columbia Poetry Review, Court Green, La Presa*, and many other journals. Born and raised in Argentina, Castro now lives in New Jersey with his partner.

Rob Colgate's poetry embodies an ekphrastic response to the environments that he has been exposed to and the social structures in which he participates. In his contributions, he attempts to explore the nuances of his own deviance – gay, brown, psychotic – as they map onto the queer experiences he is surrounded and challenged by in his daily life.

Steven Cordova's full-length collection of poetry, *Long Distance*, was published by Bilingual Review Press in 2010. His poems have appeared in *Barrow Street, Bellevue Literary Review, Callaloo, The Journal* and *Northwest Review*. He reviews fiction and nonfiction for Lambda Literary. From San Antonio, TX, he lives in Brooklyn, New York.

Alfred Corn is the author of eleven volumes of poetry, two novels, and three collections of essays. He has received a Guggenheim fellowship, an NEA, an Award in Literature from the American

Academy of Arts and Letters, and a fellowship from the Academy of American Poets. He has taught at Yale, Columbia, UCLA, the University of Cincinnati, and the University of Tulsa. He lives in Rhode Island.

Pam Crow lives in Portland, Oregon where she works as a clinical social worker. After winning the Astraea Emerging Lesbian Poets prize in 1998, she published her first book of poems, <u>Inside This House</u>, with Main Street Rag press in 2007. Her poems have appeared in *Southern Poetry Review, Calyx, Seattle Review, Ploughshares,* and other national journals. Last year she won the Neil Shepard prize for poetry from *Green Mountain Review*.

Lisa Dordal, author of *Mosaic of the Dark* from Black Lawrence Press, is a Pushcart Prize nominee and the recipient of an Academy of American Poets University Prize and the Robert Watson Poetry Prize. Her poetry has appeared in *Best New Poets, Ninth Letter*, *CALYX, The Feminist Wire,* and *Nasty Women Poets: An Unapologetic Anthology of Subversive Verse.*

Robert Fleming survived writing poetry for > 30 years. He lives in Arlington, Virginia, USA. He has been published in *Poet's Domain, Spoonfed, Radical Fairy Diary, The Watch, California Quarterly, Bay Windows, Dekalb Literary Arts Journal, Catalyst, & American Poetry Anthology.* His poetry masters are William Shakespeare, Robert Frost, E.E. Cummings, Dorothy Parker, and John Berryman.

Donna Fleischer's fourth poetry book, < *Periodic Earth* >(2016, Casa de Cinco Hermanas Press), encompasses a 20-page poem on being lesbian that was written over a span of twenty years. Her poems are in small press anthologies and journals worldwide, including *The End of the World Project, Dispatches From the Poetry Wars, Marsh Hawk Press Review, Otoliths,* and *Spiral Orb*. Her wife and she live on a traprock mountain ridge in Connecticut.

Charlotte Forrester is a Long Island based writer, political coordinator and community activist. She's been published by Bards Annual last year and works tirelessly to bring social, economic, and environmental justice for New York State. She was also instrumental for Blue Wave of 2018 when she worked as a field organizer for Anna Kaplan's Campaign for State Senate.

Tara Sidhoo Fraser lives, works and writes on the unceded territory of the Musqueam, Skxwú7mesh and Tsleil-Waututh nations AKA Vancouver, BC. Her work has appeared in Autostraddle and Anathema Magazine.

Eddy Funkhouser is a queer non-binary urban farmer and gardener from San Francisco, CA. Their work can be found in Yerba Buena Center for the Arts' Beyond Bloodlines and Written on the Body: Letters from Trans and Non-Binary Survivors of Sexual Assault and Domestic Violence.

Davidson Garrett is a poet and actor who drove a New York City yellow taxi for forty years to subsidize his artistic pursuits. A member of Actors Equity and SAG/AFTRA, his poetry and prose have been published in many literary journals. He is the author of the poetry collection, *King Lear of the Taxi* published by Advent Purple Press. Davidson is originally from Louisiana and lives in Manhattan. www.davidsongarrett.com

Tova Green began writing poetry in an English class at Music and Art High School in New York City and has turned toward poetry all her life for inspiration and as a form for expressing her concerns about the world. She is a Zen priest, lives in San Francisco, and plays cello.

Sean Hanrahan is a poet originally hailing from Dale City, Virginia. He is the author of the chapbook, Hardened Eyes on the Scan, published by Moonstone Press. His work has also been included in several anthologies and journals. He currently serves on the Moonstone Press Editorial Board and as an editor for *Toho* and instructor for the Green Street Poetry workshop.

Hanna Harris is a professional spoken word artist, organizer, and educator. She has performed her poetry at the Women's March, LACMA, Warped Tour, Dodger Stadium, TOMs, and more. Hanna is also the coach of the Los Angeles Youth Poetry Slam team and the co-organizer of #TransMarchLA.

Sandra de Helen's work appears in Artemis Journal, The Dandelion Review, The Medical Journal of Australia, Mom Egg, Lavender Review: Night Issue, The Dramatist magazine and other journals. Her collections of poetry are published by Launch Point Press. *Desire Returns for a Visit* was released November 9, 2018.

Scott Hightower is the author of four books of poetry in the US and two bilingual collections published in Madrid. He lives in Manhattan and teaches at New York University's Gallatin School of Individualized Study.

Walter Holland, PhD, is the author of three books of poetry *A Journal of the Plague Years: Poems 1979-1992*, *Transatlantic*, and *Circuit*, as well as one novel, *The March*. HIs work has appeared in *The Antioch Review*, *HazMat*, *Redivider*, *Rhino*, *Lovejets*, and many other journals and anthologies. He writes book reviews for <u>*LambdaLiterary.org*</u> and *Pleiades*. Follow him at: <u>walterhollandwriter.com</u>.

As an older queer poet, **D. Scott Humphries** writes the stories of friends who've passed in the early days of the AIDS epidemic. He considers it a matter of urgent importance, and respect, to tell the stories others are no longer able to tell themselves, to keep alive in memory those who would otherwise become ghosts, to remind later LGBT+ generations of a part of their history and those who lived it. These voices still need to be heard.

Randall Ivey's work has appeared in a number of sources, both gay and non-gay, including *Assaracus*, *Impossible Archetype*, and *The South Carolina Review*. He's the author of a novel, three story collections, and a children's book.

Collin Kelley's poetry collections include "Midnight in a Perfect World" and the American Library Association-honored "Render," both published by Sibling Rivalry Press. Kelley is also the author of the acclaimed Venus Trilogy of novels: "Conquering Venus," "Remain in Light" and "Leaving Paris."

Alexis Kennedy is a youth advocate giving young people facing mental health struggles a voice. She is the Author of "This is What it Feels Like". She enjoys taking photos and making art, you can follow her on Instagram at @bruises.to.butterflies

Sur* Landfried graduated from the University of Marburg in Germany with a BA in educational science with a focus on queer theory. Ze is transforming this focus to visual arts, queerfeminist theatre and poetry. Sur* is currently working with unaccompanied minor refugees.

A survivor of Mississippi College, **Amy Lauren** was selected as the finalist for the 2018 Gival Press Oscar Wilde Award and the 2019 Tennessee Williams Contest. Her poetry has appeared in *The Gay & Lesbian Review*, *Cordite Poetry Review*, *New Orleans Review*, and elsewhere.

David Lewis-Peart is an emerging poet and playwright. He was recipient of the Christopher Hewitt Award for poetry, Honorable Mention, and was included as a community curator for the 3rd Annual Lambda Literary Festival - Los Angeles. His writing explores grief, loss, shame, and truth-telling. David is presently completing his first book of poetry, *Pray You Break*, while undergoing writer's residencies with Buddies in Bad Times Theatre and Obsidian Theatre Company in Toronto.

R. Zamora Linmark is the author of four poetry collections, all from Hanging Loose Press, most recently *Pop Vérité*. He's also published three novels—"Rolling The R's", "Leche", and, forthcoming from Random House this August, "The Importance of Being Wilde at Heart". He divides his home between Honolulu, Hawaii, and Baguio, Philippines.

Timothy Liu's latest book is *Luminous Debris: New & Selected Legerdemain (1992-2017)*. Widely published, his accolades include the Norma Farber First Book Award from the Poetry Society of America; a Beyond Margins / Open Book Award from PEN America; and a Book-of-the-Year Award from Publishers Weekly. A reader of occult esoterica, his journals and papers are archived in the Berg

Collection at the New York Public Library. Liu divides his time between Manhattan and Woodstock, NY.

Chip Livingston is the author of the poetry collections *Museum of False Starts* and *Crow-Blue, Crow-Black*; the story collection *Naming Ceremony*; and the novel *Owls Don't Have to Mean Death*. He teaches in the low-rez MFA program at Institute of American Indian Arts. He lives in Montevideo, Uruguay.

Richard Loranger is a writer, performer, musician, visual artist, and all-around squeaky wheel, currently residing in Oakland, CA. He curates "#we", a talk and reading series of queer perspectives, and is the founder of "Poetea", a monthly literary conversation group. He is the author of three books and nine chapbooks, and has work in many magazines and journals. You can find more about his work and scandals at www.richardloranger.com.

Sassafras Lowrey is a straight-edge punk who grew up to become the 2013 winner of the Lambda Literary Emerging Writer Award. Hir books have been honored by organizations ranging from the National Leather Association to the American Library Association. Sassafras lives and writes in Portland, Oregon with hir partner, and their menagerie of dogs and cats. Learn more at www.SassafrasLowrey.com

Deirdre Maultsaid has been published in *The Barcelona Review, Canadian Women's Studies, Canthius, CV2*, the *Danforth Review, Other Voices, Pif, Prairie Fire*, the *Puritan*, and others. She is a queer writer living in Vancouver, Canada on the unceded territory of the Coast Salish People. More information at www.deirdremaultsaid.com and @deirdmaultsaid.

Savana Mazumder is a writer and graduate of the University of Massachusetts - Amherst with a degree in Linguistics and Psychology. They spend their time writing, tutoring, reading, and petting all of the dogs and cats. They hope to make the world a queerer place.

Pat McCutcheon is a retired professor who taught for thirty years at the college where, as a student, she was first encouraged to become a poet. She lives with her wife and writes in the redwoods of far northern California. Her chapbook, *Recovering Perfectionist,* was published in 1996. In 2015 a second, *Slipped Past Words,* was a winner in Finishing Line Press's Women's Voices Chapbook contest.

A resident of NY, **Stephen Mead** is an Outsider multi-media artist and writer.   Since the 1990s he's been grateful to many editors for publishing his work in print zines and eventually online. He is also grateful to have managed to keep various day jobs for the Health Insurance. For links to his writing, art and other media (and even merchandise) please feel free to Google Stephen Mead Art.

Lynn McGee is the author of the poetry collections *Tracks* (Broadstone Books, 2019) and *Sober Cooking* (Spuyten Duyvil Press, 2016), as well as two award-winning poetry chapbooks: *Heirloom Bulldog* (Bright Hill Press, 2015), and *Bonanza* (Slapering Hol Press, 1997). For more information, visit www.lynnmcgee.com.

Glenn McMurray has travelled to where he is now via a varied and rich path which includes work as a translator, life and children in Germany, sport, poetry, drama and creativity. Glenn came out a year and a half ago and is a reflective and soulful man currently living, loving and building his life in Norfolk with his beautiful family.

David Messineo is among the 25 longest-serving poetry editors and independent literary magazine publishers still active in America. For his work with *Sensations Magazine* (http://www.sensationsmag.com) since 1987, he is a three-consecutive year winner in the national American Literary Magazine Awards, and a 2009 recipient of a New Jersey State Jefferson Award for Public Service. His poetry has been published in literary magazines on four continents, and is published in nine poetry books and chapbooks: *First Impressions, Suburban Gothic, A Taste of Italy, A Taste of Brazil, Restoration, Formal, The Search for the Sapphire Robe, Historiopticon,* and *20 Minutes of Calm: Nature Poems.* He resides in northwest New Jersey, but considers Manhattan his playground and home away from home.

Michael Montlack is editor of the Lambda Finalist essay anthology *My Diva: 65 Gay Men on the Women Who Inspire Them* (University of Wisconsin Press) and author of the poetry collection *Cool Limbo*

(NYQ Books). Recently his work has appeared in *North American Review, Barrow Street, Hotel Amerika, Court Green, The Offing, Poet Lore,* and *Los Angeles Review.* His essays have appeared in *Huffington Post* and *Advocate.com.*

Louise Moore has been writing and getting published for a long time. She has recently read her work for the Los Angeles Lambda Literary Festival and for the City of West Hollywood. As our out community has grown up so have our concerns. So these poems reflect that diversity.

Tal Moskowitz is a 10-year-old transgender boy. His hobbies include playing the saxophone, swimming, playing kickball and soccer. Tal is in the fifth grade and when he grows up he would like to be an astronaut, actor or inventor.

Emmet Munroe works as a Language Arts and Drama teacher at a local middle school in Harford County, Maryland. He enjoys cooking, reading, and volunteering within the community. He is currently hard at work on his debut novel.

Joseph Munisteri is the author of the book *Butterflies in Space* and *Pantheon of Poetry* which are available for purchase on Amazon.com He also has a blog that documents the adventures of his traveling sketchbook, www.unlockcreativity.org. You can follow him on Instagram at ButterfliesIn.Space

"Be the person you needed when you were younger." **Erica Nicole** is a psychiatric nurse & nationally ranked poet who lives her life by this quote. She has found healing in poetry and hopes to facilitate healing in others through poetry. Erica Nicole is the author of *The One Who Loves Her Next, The Book That Lived,* and the co-author of *From the Outside Looking In,* a poetry collection meant to raise awareness of suicide among LGBTQ* youth. Follow Erica Nicole on social media @EricaNicolePoetry

Casey Oraa is a queer, racialized artist and activist based out of Toronto. He's the creator and writer of Champ, a queer indie comic.

When he's not working, creating or advocating, he's probably asleep. Follow along online at caseyoraa.com.

Joshua Sassoon Orol is a trans Jewish poet from Raleigh, NC, writing with the texts, tunes, and stories passed down from their mixed heritage family. Joshua completed an MFA at NC State University, and received an Academy of American Poets prize while at UNC Chapel Hill. You can read other work in recent issues of Driftwood Press, Nimrod, and Storm Cellar.

Emory Parker is an NYC-based actress/filmmaker. Her most recent narrative short, "The Perfect Fit," has screened at various festivals including ITV Fest, Golden Door International Film Festival, and Astoria Film Festival where it took home the Grand Jury Prize. Emory is a recipient of the Horizon Award and the Co-Founder of Blue Slate Films, a female-run production company that aims to bring untold stories to the forefront.

Kenneth Pobo published a book in 2017 called *Loplop in a Red City*. Forthcoming from Clare Songbirds Publishing House is a book of his prose poems called *The Antlantis Hit Parade*. His work has appeared in: *The Queer South Anthology*, *Mudfish*, *Bay Windows*, *Hawaii Review*, and elsewhere.

Michael Allen Potter is the author of *TRIFECTA: Three Very Award-Winning Gay Plays* and holds degrees in English and creative writing from Union College (NY), San Francisco State University, and The University of Iowa. His work has appeared in *Memoir Mixtapes, Ghost City Review, Art & Understanding*, and *Vallum*.

Kelly J. Powell is a graduate of the SUNY @ Binghamton's Literature and Rhetoric Program and the proud single mother of a SUNY @ Stonybrook double major and honor student. She is a poet native to Long Island and wishes to remain so. Her book *Posthumously Yours*, published by Local Gems now available, but selling out fast!!!

Anthony Radovich lives in Seattle, Washington. A queer activist, mentor, organizer, and recovery coach, he was sainted by the Sisters of Perpetual Indulgence, Abbey of St. Joan, for his work that improves the fabric of community. He writes stories and poetry with the goal to foster intergenerational connection and leadership. In December 2018, he debuted his writing in the performance event, "AIDS It's in Our Blood: Stories of Love, Loss, Rage, and Survival" at Gay City.

Barb Reynold's chapbook "Boxing Without Gloves" was published by Finishing Line Press in 2014, and her poems have appeared in numerous journals. She founded and curates the Britt Marie Poetry Series in Albany, CA, and she is currently writing a biography and filming a documentary about a lesbian relative, Margaret/Mark.

Dennis Rhodes has published three collections, most recently *The Letter I* from Chelsea Station Editions. His poems and essays have appeared in numerous literary and mainstream publications. He was a long-time resident of New York City and Provincetown, Massachusetts, both of which have been settings for his work. He currently lives in Florida.

Steven Riel is the author of one full-length collection of poetry, *Fellow Odd Fellow*, and three chapbooks, the most recent of which, *Postcard from P-town*, having been published by Seven Kitchens Press as runner-up for the inaugural Robin Becker Chapbook Prize. His poems have appeared in several anthologies and numerous periodicals. He is the editor-in-chief of the online Franco-American literary journal *Résonance*.

Matthew Roberts is studying to be an English teacher while pursuing his passion of writing. During his free time Matthew volunteers with the 4-H Program, and the Freemasons, and created a charity to promote LGBTQ+ focused publications in libraries and bookstores across the state of Maryland. Matthew also writes under the pseudonym, G. Von Prince.

Rita "Rusty" Rose is a poet who has gained recognition in the United States and abroad. She has performed her works for colleges, organizations and social programs and is a pioneer in the modern LGBT movement, having participated in the Stonewall Rebellion of 1969. In 2018 she was deemed Poet Laureate of the LGBT community on Long Island, New York. She has also received a Bards Award for Literature, 2018, and an award for Super Poem Sunday 2018.

Marc Rosen is the author of *Monster of Fifty-Nine Moons and Other Poems* (Local Gems Poetry Press, 2016), and has edited numerous poetry anthologies. He lost track of where he's been published, and does not know his full bibliography. He serves numerous disability rights organizations with distinction, and begins law school in September 2019. He has finally found his people, community, and sense of home.

Rae Rozman was a middle school English teacher who is now a school counselor in Austin, Texas. A femme dyke, her personal is political, so her poetry explores queer romantic and platonic love. She frequently writes about brain injuries and occasionally writes about her students. When she's not at work, she enjoys spending time with her long-term partner and their two rescue bunnies. You can find her on Instagram at @mistress_of_mnemosyne.

Kareena Rudra is 16 years old. She is a a queer highschooler & an active advocate in her community. She can be found online at @literate.her on Instagram and by searching "Kareena Rudra" on Youtube.

Anna Sago is a LGBT high school student living in rural Tennessee. She loves music and wants to study Journalism in college.

Jessica Saldaña grew up to the song of Mexican prayers and loud piano music on the Southside of Chicago. An all-around maker of things visual/auditory/haptic, their work is interested in power, pleasure, plurality and the relativistic velocity of queer bodies. They wield a B.A. in Music Composition, an M.A. in Performance Studies from NYU/Tisch, and will soon obtain an M.F.A. from Parsons/The New School. You can find their online devil spirit in hell_data_@instagram where they dump their songy spells.

Sarah Sarai's poems are in *Sinister Wisdom, Barrow Street, The Collagist, Boston Review* and many other journals. Her collections are *The Future Is Happy*; *That Strapless Bra in Heaven* (forthcoming 2020); *Geographies of Soul and Taffeta*. She lives in NYC.

Paula Sayword has published two books of poetry, *Canticle of Light and Dark* and *What Sleep Inside*. Her poetry has appeared in various journals and collections, including *Sinister Wisdom, Naugatuck River Review, Silkworm*, and *Adrienne Rich, a Tribute Anthology*. She lives in Western Massachusetts with her longtime woman partner.

Lois Shearing is a bisexual activist and writer. They are the founder of the Bi Survivors Network and in their free time, they enjoy crafting and reading.

Deborah Chava Singer is (still) a bisexual. Originally from San Diego, CA where she studied with the Mesa College Theatre Company and Queer Players, she now lives in Washington state. Her writing's appeared in *Chantwood, Hashtag Queer 2, Santa Fe Literary Review, The Human Touch, Cirque, Fear and Ruin, Jonathan, Off the Rocks*, and others. www.latenightawake.com

Heather Stewart is a doctoral student in Philosophy at the University of Western Ontario in Canada, though her home is down south in Kentucky. Heather researches and writes on a variety of ethical issues, particular those impacting LGBTQ+ communities. She is recently working on the concept and mechanisms of "bisexual erasure."

F Cade Swanson is a dad, a published writer, and a former Fulbright scholar. He grew up in Virginia, loves the ocean, and runs a community center in Seattle.

Seth Walker ranked among the top slam poets in the world for years as he toured around the U.S. & eventually won the I.W.P.S. Slam Champion of Denver, Colorado's world famous Cafe NUBA, later taking 4th in the world in 2012. He has been on several national slam teams, won countless titles & awards, & spoken before colleges & universities across the nation. Seth has now taken to a less-truck-based lifestyle & is enjoying living in an undisclosed location as a playwright & lecturer.

Mark Ward is the author of *Circumference* (Finishing Line Press, 2018). He was the Poet Laureate for *Glitterwolf* and his work has appeared in *The Irish Times, Poetry Ireland Review, Skylight47, Assaracus, Tincture* and more. New work is out/forthcoming from *Peculiar, Softblow, Wussy* and the anthology, *Lovejets: Queer Male Poets on 200 Years of Walt Whitman.* He lives in Dublin, Ireland and is the founding editor of *Impossible Archetype,* a journal of LGBTQ+ poetry. He is currently working on his first full-length collection, *Nightlight.*

Julene Tripp Weaver is a psychotherapist and writer in Seattle, WA. Her latest poetry book, *truth be bold—Serenading Life & Death in the Age of AIDS*, was a finalist for the Lambda Literary Awards and won the Bisexual Book Award. Her work is online at *The Seattle Review of Books, HIV Here & Now, Voices in the Wind, Antinarrative Journal*; more of her writing can be found at www.julenetrippweaver.com.

Rick Allen Wilson is a writer, producer, educator, and musician. His produced plays include *Too Much, Too Far, Too Soon, The Declaration: a parable of same-sex marriage* and *Hockey: the musical!* Mr. Wilson is a Harvard Club Outstanding Educator and Vice President of the Board of Directors of Long Island Crisis Center, with special interest in shepherding Pride For Youth, Long Island's oldest LGBT service organization. rickallenwilson.com

Daniel J. Zyzniewski writes poems and drama plays; one of his poems about love, "Beachhead Dune" was published in *Scene & Heard Journal* (Valentine's Day 2018); one of his poems, "Mind-electrification" was published in *LPC Literary Anthology Havik: Rise* by Las Positas College, Livermore, California, 2018;

Local Gems Poetry Press is a small Long Island, NY based poetry press dedicated to spreading poetry through performance and the written word. Local Gems believes that poetry is the voice of the people, and as the sister organization of the Bards Initiative, believes that poetry can be used to make a difference.

Local Gems Press has published over 200 titles.

www.localgemspoetrypress.com

60428543R00185

Made in the USA
Columbia, SC
16 June 2019